Sustaining Local Food Webs

Sustaining Local Food Webs

Edited by Ben Murphy

PRACTICAL ACTION
Publishing

Practical Action Publishing Ltd
The Schumacher Centre, Bourton on Dunsmore, Rugby, Warwickshire, CV23 9QZ, UK
www.practicalactionpublishing.org

ISBN 978-1-85339-880-3 Hardback
ISBN 978-1-85339-881-0 Paperback
ISBN 978-1-78044-880-0 Library Ebook

Citation: Murphy, Ben (2015) *Sustaining Local Food Webs*, Rugby, UK: Practical Action Publishing,
<http://dx.doi.org/10.3362/9781780448800>

Contributors:
Gustave Ewole (PROPAC)
Mamadou Goïta (ROPPA)
Stephen Muchiri (EAFF)
Babacar Ndao (ROPPA)
EAFF, PROPAC and ROPPA are members of the europAfrica campaign
Graeme Willis (Campaign for the Protection of Rural England)

Since 1974, Practical Action Publishing has published and disseminated books and information in
support of international development work throughout the world. Practical Action Publishing is a
trading name of Practical Action Publishing Ltd (Company Reg. No. 1159018), the wholly owned
publishing company of Practical Action. Practical Action Publishing trades only in support of its
parent charity objectives and any profits are covenanted back to Practical Action (Charity Reg. No.
247257, Group VAT Registration No. 880 9924 76).

Cover photo: Vendors selling vegetables at the central market, Njemena, Chad. ©FAO/Carl de
Souza
Printed by Latimer Trend, United Kingdom

Contents

Foreword

This book is a tribute to those who feed us – the small-scale food providers who supply the local food webs that nourish more than 70 per cent of the world's population. It is a timely contribution to the contested discourse about how healthy food supplies can be secured for future generations.

The main message of this book is that food webs are productive, resilient and healthy, connecting food providers and consumers locally. These food webs are efficient in terms of food provision when compared with the long chains that deliver the commodities produced by industrial agriculture to distant consumers. Local food webs need protection, increased investment and support.

This message is directed to those who influence agricultural, food and nutrition policies, urging them to invest in those who currently feed the majority of the people in the continent – Africa's family farmers – and to transform European policies so that they can regenerate healthy local food webs, with minimal negative impact on Africa and other continents.

The report has been prepared and published with resources from the campaign *europAfrica: towards food sovereignty*. This is a coalition of European civil society organisations and African farmers' regional networks, in West, Central and East Africa, working together for mutually supportive and sustainable food systems in Europe and Africa. They act together on major current issues concerning food and agricultural policies and related trade, environment and development cooperation issues. europAfrica aims to raise awareness and advocate on shared issues and to promote sustainable, ecological and biodiverse small-scale family farming and local agri-food systems that bring consumers and producers closer together. The campaign supports the realisation of food sovereignty both in Africa and in Europe. Food sovereignty is a framework which includes the right for people and communities to define their own food and agricultural policies, without impeding the food sovereignty of others. europAfrica's partners in the United Kingdom are Practical Action with the UK Food Group. europAfrica is co-financed by the European Union.

The report is based on contributions, interviews and papers prepared by representatives of the African Farmers' Regional Networks – Mamadou Goïta and Babacar Ndao (ROPPA), Gustave Ewole (PROPAC), and Stephen Muchiri (EAFF) – and several local food projects in the UK and Hungary. In addition, the report of the African Farmers' Regional Networks meeting in Yaoundé is annexed. This summarises the demands of Africa's family farmers for improvements in investment policy in support of family farming and local markets. It was an important contribution to the debates on agricultural investment in the UN Committee on World Food Security and FAO. Also annexed is a methodology for mapping local food webs developed by Graeme Willis and colleagues from the Campaign for the Protection of Rural England – a useful tool for assessing the contribution of local food webs to food provision. Drawing on all this information, previous europAfrica reports and food sovereignty processes in which europAfrica participates, Ben Murphy has produced this informative report. The UK Food Group thanks everyone who made a direct or indirect contribution, and for their patience and commitment, and hopes that this report provides an adequate reflection of the dynamic local food regime they defend and promote.

As presented in this report, the experiences and demands of those who provide food locally are compelling. Readers will want to endorse its final statement: 'Local food webs are a cornerstone for the model of food provision that should be prioritised in order to secure our future food.'

Patrick Mulvany
UK Food Group

Abbreviations and acronyms

AFSI	Aquila Food Security Initiative
AGRA	Alliance for a Green Revolution in Africa
ARD	Agricultural Research for Development
AU	African Union
CAADP	The Comprehensive Africa Agriculture Development Programme
CAP	Common Agricultural Policy
CFA	Central African franc
CFS	Committee on World Food Security
CNCR	Conseil National de Concertation et de coopération des Ruraux, Sénégal
CNOP	Coordination Nationale des Organisations Paysannes du Mali
CPRE	Campaign to Protect Rural England
CSA	Community Supported Agriculture
CSM	civil society mechanism
CSOs	civil society organisations
EAC	East African Community
EAFF	Eastern Africa Farmers' Federation
EPAs	Economic Partnership Agreements
EQM	Environmental Quality Mark
EU	European Union
FAO	Food and Agriculture Organization of the United Nations
FDI	foreign direct investment
FO	farmers' organisation
IAASTD	International Assessment of Agricultural Knowledge, Science and Technology for Development (international agricultural assessment)
ICIPE	International Centre for Insect Physiology and Ecology
IFAD	International Fund for Agricultural Development
KENFAPP	Kenya National Federation of Agricultural Producers
KSh	Kenyan shilling
KSSFF	Kenya Small Scale Farmers Forum
NGO	non-governmental organisation
NEPAD	New Partnership for Africa's Development
NHS	National Health Service (UK)
ODA	official development assistance
PAFO	Pan-African Farmers' Organisation
PROPAC	Plateforme Régionale des Organisations Paysannes d'Afrique Centrale
ROPPA	Réseau Des Organisations Paysannes and Producteurs de l'Afrique de l'Ouest
SACAU	Southern African Confederation of Agricultural Unions
SZÖVET	Alliance for the Living Tisza
SSA	Sub-Saharan Africa
UNCTAD	United Nations Conference on Trade and Development
UMAGRI	Union Maghrébine des Agriculteurs
WHO	World Health Organization
WTO	World Trade Organization

1
Introduction

We will strengthen our interconnecting rural – urban food webs [and] shorten distances between food provider and consumer.

Forum for People's Food Sovereignty Now! Rome, 2009

Local production provides food for 70 per cent of all people around the world, and secures a livelihood for well over 2 billion people (ETC Group 2009; see Box 1.1). The distance between producer and consumer is for most people geographically and culturally short – with food and labour shared between families, neighbours, villages, and towns. Processing and marketing may take place on the farm, in a local market, or through local businesses, in a system of interdependence and mutual reward, with up to a five-fold increase in added value for the local economy.

Box 1.1 Local food: the numbers

Eighty-five per cent of the world's food is grown and consumed – if not within the '100 mile diet' – within national borders and/or the same eco-regional zone. Most of this food is grown from peasant-bred seed which does not need the industrial agribusiness chain's synthetic fertilisers. Peasants breed and nurture 40 livestock species and almost 8000 breeds. Peasants also breed 5000 domesticated crops and have donated more than 1.9 million plant varieties to the world's gene banks. Small-scale artisanal fishers harvest and protect more than 15,000 freshwater species and many more in coastal fisheries. The work of peasants and pastoralists maintaining soil fertility is 18 times more valuable than the synthetic fertilisers provided by the seven largest corporations.

There are 1.5 billion peasants on 380 million farms; 800 million more growing urban gardens; 410 million gathering the hidden harvest of our forests and savannahs; 190 million pastoralists and well over 100 million artisanal fishers. At least 370 million of these are indigenous peoples. Together these small-scale food providers and their families make up almost half the world's population and they grow at least 70 per cent of the world's food. Better than anyone else, they feed the hungry. If we are all to eat in 2050 we will need all of them and all of their diversity.

Source: ETC Group 2009

The knowledge and expertise of those closest to the local environment is used in growing crops and vegetables, raising livestock, and catching fish, and is passed down from generation to generation. Control over the whole process of producing and providing nutritious food is held at the level of small-scale food providers, enabling them to produce the food needed by their families and communities, with surpluses for a wider market, while making viable livelihoods from their labour and protecting their local environment.

Despite feeding and employing so many, in the second half of the 20th century, local food production became increasingly eclipsed by another model of production. In many developing countries – where agriculture remains the principal activity of the rural population – under global pressure for the industrialisation of agriculture, livestock and fisheries, food provision for local consumption was being largely ignored by governments, policymakers, the private sector and donors in favour of the production and export of food and non-food commodities. At the other end of that food chain, the mass marketing of perennially available 'new' and 'cheaper' foods in all locations, from large conurbations to rural villages, has nearly eclipsed local food production. Knowledge, understanding, and skills for food production have been lost, and many of the remaining small-scale food providers are bound into unprofitable and unequal relationships with corporate buyers. The industrial food chain, starting on intensive commercial farms and their outgrowers, livestock factories and rapacious industrial fishing vessels and ending in supermarkets, provides only about 30 per cent of the food consumed globally. Yet it is inordinately profitable for the handful of corporations that provide inputs and that control markets, agricultural research, the most productive land, patents and other restrictive property rights and technologies on plant and animal species, and which also have strong lobbying powers over national governments (ETC Group 2009).

The commercial success of global agribusiness has created costs across the span of its activities: for small-scale producers and their families – many of whom are marginalised to the point that they cannot feed themselves; and consumers, more than 1 billion of whom, living in developed countries and, increasingly, in emerging economies, are obese (IFAD 2002). With so much food already produced locally, the quantity provided through the industrial system far exceeds the extra demand and the required calorie intake of those able to buy it. With the emphasis on profit, people are encouraged to consume more, leading to a doubling of obesity prevalence worldwide between 1980 and 2008 and a pandemic of Type 2 diabetes (WHO 2011). It is the imperatives of the global food industry that have brought about this incongruous situation.

For most of the last 50 years, this shift from local to global control, from the food and livelihood needs of the many to the profit of the few, has passed almost by stealth. In recent years, however, various events and projections have shaken perceptions about the sustainability of, and equity in, the provision of the food on our plates. The global food price crisis in 2008 exposed the fragility of the global food system; landgrabs for biofuels and other commodities (especially in Africa), increasing oil prices, speculative trading on food prices, and drought in grain-producing countries combined to increase the price of food commodities to the highest level since the 1980s. The food price crisis also exposed the 'losers' built into the system, as price increases in grain, wheat, and many other food products led to increasing difficulties for the poorest who are trapped by the food chain. Greater understanding about climate change, population growth, falling water supplies, and peak oil, phosphorous and land availability, along with subsequent famines in Africa and increasing obesity worldwide, have further awakened consciousness around the world that the global food system is dysfunctional (Mulvany and Ensor 2011).

Solutions from small-scale food providers

In this tumultuous time, concern is growing around securing future food supplies. For agribusiness, meeting this challenge entails acquiring new production sites, often in developing countries, co-opting more farmers into market chains, and the intensification of production through increased application of synthetic products. Millions of small-scale food producers and the organisations working with them are well aware, however, of the inequities and damages caused by the industrial model. They see a greater extension of agribusiness as deepening their marginalisation

---

Box 1.2 Local food and Food Sovereignty

Local food systems are valued in the **Food Sovereignty** policy framework, which defines the vision of small-scale food providers – peasants / family farmers, pastoralists, artisanal fisherfolk, indigenous peoples, landless peoples, rural workers, migrants, pastoralists, forest communities, women, youth, consumers and environmental and urban movements. At the Nyéléni 2007: Forum for Food Sovereignty that was held in Mali more than 500 representatives from over 80 countries agreed that food sovereignty represented the principles of a food system which:

Focuses on food for people, putting the right to food at the centre of food, agriculture, livestock and fisheries policies, and rejects the proposition that food is just another commodity or component for international agribusiness;

Values food providers and respects their rights, and rejects those policies, actions and programmes that undervalue them, threaten their livelihoods and eliminate them;

Localises food systems, bringing food providers and consumers closer together, and rejects governance structures, agreements and practices that depend on and promote unsustainable and inequitable international trade and give power to remote and unaccountable corporations;

Puts control locally over territory, land, grazing, water, seeds, livestock and fish populations, and rejects the privatisation of natural resources through laws, commercial contracts and intellectual property rights regimes;

Builds knowledge and skills that conserve, develop and manage localised food production and harvesting systems; and rejects technologies that undermine, threaten or contaminate these, e.g. genetic engineering;

Works with nature in diverse, agroecological production and harvesting methods that maximise ecosystem functions and improve resilience and adaptation, especially in the face of climate change, and rejects energy-intensive industrialised methods which damage the environment and contribute to global warming.

Source: Nyéléni 2007

In order to achieve this, local, small-scale food providers and consumers, and their organisations, must be at the centre of decision-making on food issues. Control over territory, land, grazing, water, seeds, livestock and fish populations is placed in the hands of local food providers and respects their rights. Producing food in harmony with the ecology has high (often family) labour requirements but minimises use of other external inputs (irrigation water, chemicals, seeds), and maximises: the use of local knowledge and innovation systems; the diversity of locally adapted seeds and breeds used for food; and ecosystem functions, which support plants and animals and provide environmental services, within biocultural landscapes.

Source: UK Food Group 2010

Local, small-scale food providers and consumers must be at the centre of decision-making on food issues

into poverty and worsening the environmental impacts, further undermining the natural resources that food production relies on. In order to eradicate hunger now and meet the food needs of a further 2 billion people by 2050, they are calling for a re-evaluation of where the food that feeds most people in the world comes from, the local knowledge and expertise that makes this possible, the ways in which the environment can be preserved through more ecological farming techniques, and the hardships faced by the numerous and varied actors in local food webs (See Box 1.2).

The ability of small-scale producers within local food webs to produce adequate, nutritious food while preserving the natural environment has received high-level recognition. In 2011, the UN Special Rapporteur for the Right to Food released a report detailing how agroecology, practised by small-scale food providers, can help to raise productivity, reduce rural poverty, improve nutrition, adapt to climate change, and protect agricultural biodiversity and related ecosystem functions building on the best local agricultural practices (De Schutter 2011). In the report, the central role of small-scale food producers in providing local food is clear:

> Agroecology is highly knowledge-intensive, based on techniques that are not delivered top-down but developed on the basis of farmers' knowledge and experimentation [...] The participation of farmers is vital for the success of agroecological practices. So far, agroecology has been developed by grassroots organisations and NGOs, and it has spread through farmer field schools and farmers' movements, such as the Campesino a Campesino movement in Central America. Experience with agroecological techniques is growing everyday within peasant networks. (De Schutter 2011)

In their challenge for a fairer and less harmful food system, actors within local food webs around the world are making their case heard. Innovative ways of harnessing their collective power are being adopted, aiding producers, processors and sellers, and attracting consumers back into an engagement with food production. Social movements, organisations of small-scale food providers, non-governmental organisations (NGOs) and some scientific organisations are also campaigning and raising awareness about this sustainable model of food provision.

This report captures the spirit of this movement for local food webs. It sets out to demonstrate the value and challenges of local, resilient, biodiverse and productive food systems that would benefit from greater support and compliant policies. It uses examples from five countries across Africa and Europe, yet has relevance across all continents, demonstrating how productive local food systems can improve small-scale family farming and reduce hunger, in contrast to industrial agricultural systems. This report is produced as part of the europAfrica campaign, a coalition of civil society organisations and African farmers' regional networks working together for a mutually supportive and sustainable agriculture in Europe and Africa.

Layout of the report

The first section explores the African context. Agriculture provides a livelihood for 70 per cent of the population in Africa and small-scale food provision, mainly by women, provides food for 80 per cent of the population.

Africa is often diagnosed as a continent deficient in the trappings of the agro-industrial model, and a new market for commercial agricultural products. In the first chapter, from Cameroon, local food production and exchange is shown to be an integral part of the informal economy, and a lifeline during the failings of

4

the formal sector. The following chapter is from Kenya, where agribusinesses own much of the high potential land available and small-scale producers are pushed to the margins. Nevertheless, the examples from Kenya show how local food webs are key to food provision for the majority. In the following chapter on Mali, Mamadou Goïta, executive secretary of the West African farmers' network ROPPA, gives a first-hand account of how farmers and governments can resist the encroachment of agribusiness.

Europe's food system, the focus of the second section, is by contrast heavily industrialised and concentrated in the hands of relatively few large-scale commercial farmers, although there are many others who grow food at smaller scales and also grow food non-commercially. The introduction of the Common Agricultural Policy (CAP) in 1963 has drastically reduced the number of farms and farmers by providing incentives that facilitate concentration into larger farms, and by increasingly reducing the economic viability of those that do not sell up. Now, '6 per cent of the cereal farms produce 60 per cent of the total European cereal production' and '90 per cent of poultry production is in the hands of 10 per cent of producers' (Calza Bini and Boccaleoni 2010). Despite this, Europe has not lost the desire to have smaller family-run farms and is home to numerous movements challenging not only the CAP but also hyper-capitalism and the negative environmental and health impacts of agribusiness. The chapter from England takes one tool used in this campaign – the mapping of local food webs – to demonstrate the value that interdependent local food actors bring to six regions of the country. The following chapter from Hungary showcases three initiatives that have developed and maintained flourishing alternatives to the country's encroaching large-scale commercial sector with its subsequent negative environmental impacts.

While the relative economic levels of the agricultural sectors of Europe and Africa, and the affluence of their populations, are very different, the two continents do share similarities in terms of threats, and they have mutual impacts on each other's

---

Box 1.3 The agro-industrial model

The antithesis of local food webs is the industrial model of commodity production. Industrialised production of crops, livestock and fish, and the associated processing, global distribution and retailing of these commodities, operates on a scale that dwarfs the barter and exchange systems, farmers' markets, and community-supported family farms in Africa and Europe. Industrial monocrops are intensively farmed on areas of land tens or hundreds of times larger than the typical family farm, using high volumes of chemical inputs and compliant seeds, and techniques to minimise labour on the farm often with scant regard to environmental health. Similarly, livestock factories using mainly imported feed and with poor animal welfare standards are a hallmark of the industrial system. The outputs are commodities – foodstuffs, horticultural products, agrofuels and biomass – usually transported over large distances as part of national and international supply chains. Industrialised production is based on a perverse system of economic rewards which benefit a few corporations at the expense of the livelihoods of most farmers and the food needs of the majority. It can be applied at different scales. In the 1960s–70s the so-called 'Green Revolution' introduced industrial-style production methods at smaller scales, generating yield increases of food commodities (wheat, rice, maize) but at costs of sustainability, the environment and livelihoods.

The environmental legacy of this production system – destroyed agricultural biodiversity and eroded soils, depletion and contamination of water supplies – undermines the natural resources upon which agriculture relies. In addition, the carbon used in, and generated by, industrial commodity production and harvesting is a major contributor to climate change.

food systems. Agricultural and export subsidies in the European Union (EU) can lead to the 'dumping' of produce below the costs of local production on African markets. Africa provides Europe with many temperate fresh foods, out of season in the European winter, as well as supplies of tropical foods and commodities. At the same time, the EU and individual member states support the Comprehensive African Agricultural Development Programme (CAADP) as part of the Africa–EU strategy and have an agreed policy on food security for development with which all other EU policies should be coherent.

Africa

Family farms produce up to 80% of the food consumed in African countries, much of which does not enter the formal market. They provide employment for 70% of the population, both directly and by stimulating local economies, and constitute the only potential solution for absorbing the growing population of unemployed young people. They use a large proportion of cultivated, fallow and grazed land and are responsible for the sustainable management of the bulk of Africa's natural resources. They constitute a response to the risks of food price volatility.

Synthesis report of African Farmers' Regional Networks meeting in Yaoundé (see Annex 2)

African food and agriculture has grabbed the world's attention: in any European supermarket fruits, vegetables, coffee, flowers and other goods grown in the most productive lands of the continent can be found. Development programmes, donors, and private companies encourage farmers into export markets, while selling them new inputs and providing the infrastructure that will make this possible. Asian and Middle Eastern entities are buying up large tracts of land to acquire the natural resources that they lack for their food security, and European companies are doing the same for the production of non-food products, such as biofuels (Aubry et al. 2012). This is not to mention the many regional and national programmes within Africa concerned with boosting the region's GDP through agriculture. In all this, the value that a female farmer in, for example, Bafoussam, Cameroon, has in feeding her family and the wider population is lost; she is either ignored, pushed off her land, derided as a peasant, or pressured into more 'profitable' export activities.

This section highlights how the food produced by small-scale, family farms feeds the majority of people in African countries. Using examples from Cameroon, Kenya, and Mali, it focuses on how this food is produced across the continent's varied ecological zones, and the local food webs, exchange links, and support systems which facilitate commitment to a reliable local supply. From this re-evaluation of the contribution of local food providers emerges the persistent challenges faced by those who are responsible for fulfilling food needs. Their activities are vital for the continent to feed itself. Yet the present system, and the focus of those profiting from the exploitation of African farming, does not allow small-scale farmers sufficient reward for their endeavours. Without support, acknowledgement, or protection of their work, the onset of environmental hazards such as drought, diseases and pests can trigger famine and destitution in areas of many countries, especially those in conflict, as demonstrated by the persistent crises in the Horn of Africa, for example.

These events put a strain on the supply of food and challenge the local food webs built around it. However, the culture and community traditions at the heart of the production of food have remained resilient in adversity and have proved to be vital support mechanisms that have been in place for generations. In this section they are shown to be excellent alternatives for channelling greater and new support for making livelihoods more sustainable, without having to abandon the traditional role small-scale farming plays in meeting the food needs of the continent.

2 Cameroon

The food system in Cameroon thrives on local and interpersonal relations, beginning with family farmers growing crops and tending to livestock around the household. The food produced from gardens and farms is exchanged at roadsides, in local, rural and urban markets, and even across the borders with similar communities in neighbouring countries. Agriculture in Cameroon, having evolved from the export focus of the colonial period, through the varying state policies since independence in the 1960s, is today still predominantly made up of small-scale, family farms which provide 70-80 per cent of the food consumed within the county. These local food networks function largely outside the official economy, are mainly run by women entrepreneurs, and offer a livelihood for those afflicted by, or marginal to, public and private development. They function despite low attention and support; yet, as 55 per cent of the rural population in Cameroon live in poverty, there is a clear need to better reward these principal food providers – who after all serve the majority of the population.

Farmers and informal food webs

Cameroon's informal food sector became a lifeline for a high percentage of the population during the financial crisis in the mid-1980s, when high unemployment, drastic drops in income, and the decline of the national currency forced many into poverty. At the same time, the government implemented an externally-imposed Structural Adjustment Programme lasting until 1998, which removed public spending in education, agriculture, health, and infrastructure, and increased the cost of basic services. The country's food production was hit particularly hard in this period and supply fell as a consequence. In response to job losses, the removal of social benefits, and increased expense of services, households diversified their income through self-employment. Among the many products and services sold outside of the official economy, food produced and traded by small-scale family farmers became vital for mitigating the impact of the recession.

Women play the most significant role in the informal food economy, despite being hit the hardest by the financial crisis and subject to social and familial burdens. To mitigate the losses in household income, women grew more subsistence crops, and branched out into the processing, marketing, and selling of foods such as fresh fruits, vegetables, plantain, cassava or manioc, cocoyams, potatoes, beans, and maize, while also maintaining the household and meeting the family's needs (Fonjong and Endeley 2004). Female farmers today make up 75 per cent of the agricultural labour in Cameroon and, as men are typically employed on cash crop production or non-agricultural work, the women produce the vast majority of the food consumed (Mehra and Rojas 2008).

The female food entrepreneurs within Cameroon's informal food economy are commonly known as 'buyam-sellams', a name referring to those who grow crops for sale in rural markets, and the wholesale buyers transporting the produce for sale in urban areas and other rural markets. The majority of farmers sell locally, and within their division, either by taking their goods to the village market, or to women wholesalers collecting from the sides of rural roads. A third group by-passes the 'buyam-sellams' and sells their produce directly to urban dwellers (ibid.). There is sufficient local demand for the women's produce, yet farmers are often constrained by the distance they can travel with their produce; some because they transport crops by foot in wheelbarrows and head-baskets, whilst many women are further restricted by familial duties to locations near their household.

Getting food to market in general can be difficult in Cameroon. Suppliers and buyers often face lengthy transactions, police charges, and expenses in transporting food, and collecting a family's production from small weekly markets or the front door of the family home is time consuming. Despite this, local markets do not suffer from a narrow customer base, and family farmers reach consumers from far and wide because of the willingness of both buyers and sellers to travel to markets. A survey of Fako Division reveals that most customers come from out of the area and even out of the country. In Bolifamba, a town in the south-west of the country, 92 per cent of customers in the local markets (Muea, Ekona, Mile 16, Mutegene and Soppo) come from Douala, the financial capital, 50 kilometres away (Fonjong and Endeley 2004).

As in many African countries, towns have become the main pole of consumption because urban population growth and low-income housing in and around the major conurbations in recent years has reduced the availability of peri-urban farming spaces. There is much urban agriculture, particularly of maize and traditional leafy vegetables and small stock, but the 54 per cent of the population residing in Cameroon's towns and cities are more reliant on food production in neighbouring rural areas. The three large markets in Douala rely particularly on farmers from the neighbouring Moungo District. Yaoundé, the country's capital, has four large markets – Mokolo, Mfoundi, Mvog-Mbi and Essos – which sell produce from the rural areas largely for consumption by the city's population, although some is bought for re-sale in other towns.

An in-depth study of rural–urban food linkages in Cameroon plots the provenance of the estimated 50,000 cubic metric tonnes of fresh cassava roots consumed in Yaoundé in 2002. The 15 markets selling cassava are served by approximately 30,000 producers, predominantly women, commercializing in relatively small quantities (250-500 kg per trip to the market), and relying on public transport in small vehicles carrying both passengers and farm produce (Bopda et al. 2010). The women came from 110 supply villages, the most important located within a 1–4 hour radius, and bringing a range of products for sale in the markets (ibid.). Farmers

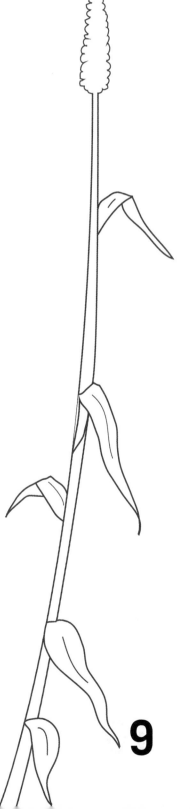

Female farmers today make up 75% of the agricultural labour in Cameroon

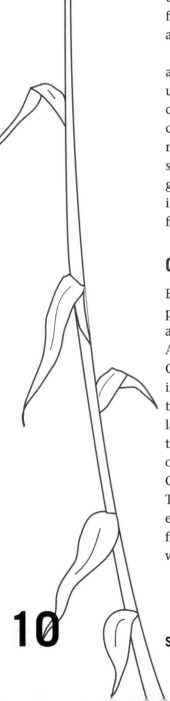

make contact with drivers before harvest and some only a day before travelling. Some notify passing vehicles by waving a white flag (ibid.).

Once in the urban markets, the food is bought by householders, restaurants, hotels and other food outlets, or is transported on to other towns. The informal sector still has an important role in providing a secure food supply for the urban population. Food vendors are very popular in the towns and cities of Cameroon for serving hot and cold foods at convenient locations. Once again, this section of the country's food provision is almost entirely operated by women. In Kumba, a central commercial town, there are 1600 vendors selling food – one for every 125 people – and 85 per cent are female-owned and run (Acho-Chi 2002). Produce – such as cocoyams, yams, cassava, grains, beans, rice, vegetables, spices, chicken, fish, and red and game meat – is brought from nearby markets, processed within the home, and transported to individual stalls, largely on foot and with a head-basket or truck-push (ibid.). Typical dishes on sale include: *mbombo djobi* (mashed cassava/fish/spices) and *kwakoko/mbanga* soup (crushed taro/palm oil/fresh fish) and *ndole* (bitter leaf soup/tubers). On average, each food vendor has over 230 customers daily and earns approximately CFA10,000 a month (US$21.98), over 400 times the legal minimum wage (ibid.). Although there are concerns about the hygiene of food processing within urban Kumba, customers patronise the vendors because of the quality of the food, their proximity to workplaces, and the ability to purchase food on credit, making the vendors a good source of nutrition for the urban poor and of convenience for the formal sector (ibid.).

Though welcome, the demand from urban areas is shaping the character of rural agricultural systems. Although there are no markets selling cassava exclusively, urban markets are gradually specialising in wholesale provision of foods, particularly cocoyams and plantains. This has improved the coordination between farmers and consumers and has made supply more efficient and reliable. Yet the draw of urban markets and wholesalers is gradually concentrating rural production in certain sectors and markets so that entire agricultural areas are becoming specialised in guaranteeing the supplies of a particular product. This may stimulate an increase in the productivity of individual crops, but, if not balanced with alternative crops, farmers run the risk of reducing productivity and agricultural biodiversity.

Cameroon's border markets

Beyond their vital importance for domestic supply of food, Cameroon's family farms play an inter-regional role within West Africa, as the informal food networks stretch across the borders into the seven neighbouring counties (Nigeria, Chad, Central African Republic, Congo, Gabon, Equatorial Guinea, and Sao Tome e Principe). Cameroon sits at the heart of this exchange, with 15 border markets located mainly in the north, south and east (see Table 2.1). These spaces for commercial transactions between producers, traders, and wholesale merchants from the region are largely informal and their activities often are not officially recognised. However, the few studies of the border market trade suggest that 'in 2008 a volume of just over 155,000 tonnes of agricultural and horticultural commodities shipped from Cameroon to its neighbours' passed through these markets (Nkendah 2010). Tomatoes, plantains, fruits, vegetables, and beans are the most common items exported out of the country at border markets, and, in return, Cameroon receives food produce from farmers in other agroecological zones, providing its population with a supply of products that it is unable to grow within the country. Because of its

10

Table 2.1 Cameroon's border markets

Market or border points	Province	Division	Sub-division	Border with
Abang-Minko'o	South	Ntem valley	Olamze	Gabon
Kye-ossi	South	Ntem valley	Olamze	Gabon, E. Guinea
Aboulou	South	Dja et Lobo	Ma'an	Gabon
Idenau	South-west	Fako		E. Guinea
Garoua-Boulaï	East	Lom et Djerem	Garoua-Boulaï	CAR
Mouloundou	East	Boumba et Ngoko	Mouloundou	CAR, Congo
Kenzo	East	Kadey	Bombe	CAR
Kousseri	Far-north	Logone et Chari	Goulfey	Nigeria
Amchide	Far-north	Mayo sava		Chad, Nigeria
Mbaîboum	North	Mayo rey	Touboro	CAR, Chad
Port peschaud	Littoral	Wouri		Gabon, E. Guinea

Source: Nkendah 2010

relative agricultural success, the produce of smallholders is helping to lessen food insecurity in the region in general, and in Gabon and Guinea Bissau in particular.

The crossroad town of Kye Ossi, in the southern region of Ntem, is home to a large border market linking north-east Equatorial Guinea and north-west Gabon. The market is open daily and provides storage facilities, modern toilets, health, security and information centres for farmers and traders. Food is traded alongside many manufactured and clothing products. The market at Abang Minko, in the south, has the reputation of being a 'world market' because it stocks the wide range of 'treasures' from Cameroon's smallholder production – plantain, cassava, onions, tomatoes, macabo, peppers, groundnuts, potatoes, and other fruits and vegetables. Between Cameroon and Nigeria, the most commonly traded goods are bush mango, kola, bitter kola, ebaye, and kutu (different species of wild mushrooms), all of which are used by local traders (FAO 2010).

As with many of the functions of the informal food economy, the border markets operate with a large degree of trust. Most transactions are made in cash using the CFA franc (the common currency shared by Cameroon and the seven surrounding states). Customers are often allowed to buy on credit, taking their purchases and paying at a later date or in instalments. Trust is built on the social cohesion of people using the markets; a high percentage of the traders live in or around the border markets, and most customers and producers are regulars, family, friends, and/or people that live nearby. In a study of the border market with Equatorial Guinea and Gabon, only 3 per cent and 5 per cent of the markets' traders respectively complained of non-payment (Nkendah 2010). Both traders and buyers have little recourse to litigation should a transaction go awry, yet the ability to lend keeps the markets operating and creates a degree of flexibility which reduces the likelihood that food will be wasted because of economic restraints.

Cameroon's food webs

The smallholder farmers, and their informal networks involved in the supply of food, play an important role in meeting food and livelihoods needs in Cameroon. But there are disadvantages and limitations of operating to such an extent outside the formal sector. Being unacknowledged in official records prevents recognition of the role that small-scale producers play in the country's food supply. This problem

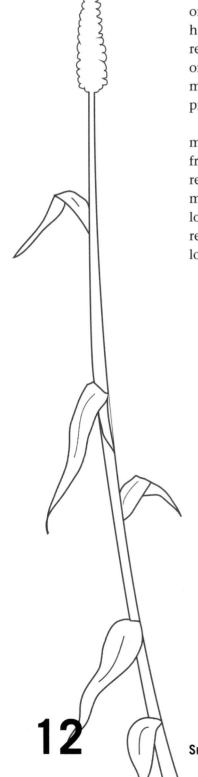

is most pronounced for women, who do the bulk of the agricultural work and already have a low social and political presence. Without recognition of their contribution to the economy and food supplies, many producers fall outside the ambit of necessary policies and support systems that could improve the conditions or efficiency of their work. Women's proximity to the household whilst producing, marketing, and processing food blurs the distinction between public and private roles, and increases their workload without extra remuneration. Going unrecognised hinders the chance of attaining support measures to relieve their burden. Nor are those who transport and market food covered by proper legislation and they are often subject to harassment from police and others on travel routes and in the urban areas, and from customs officers at the borders.

Access to information for the rural population is quite problematic. Entire areas of Cameroon are still without access to telephone, radio or television. Consequently, producers face delays in selling and buying, and there is little clarity or knowledge about market conditions and prices. Some of the border markets do have information and communication points, yet, in the main, producers do not receive the relevant and timely information that can help them make the most of their production and sales. Because of this gap, the salesmen and other intermediaries with greater information about market conditions are able to exploit producers by buying at lower prices.

Furthermore, while the Cameroonian population does an excellent job of meeting its own food needs, its ability to profit from this is constantly under pressure from external sources. The large quantities of imports into the country (nearly reaching CFA500 bn a year), of rice in particular, and the dumping of processed meat products, such as chicken pieces from the EU, have had adverse impacts on local Cameroon markets. These are being overcome through government action, restricting imports of chicken parts, and international agricultural aid to boost local rice production.

3 Kenya

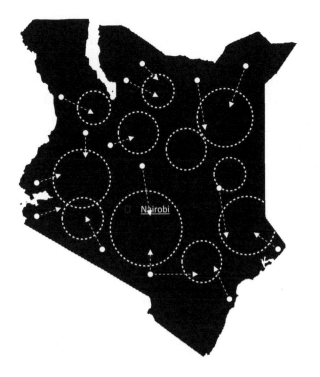

Poverty seems a paradox in a country that has one of the best-developed economies in eastern Africa. Kenya has relatively advanced agricultural and industrial sectors and substantial foreign exchange earnings from agricultural exports and tourism. Yet it is a low-income country and ranks 128th among 169 countries in the United Nations Development Programme's Human Development Index, which measures development in terms of life expectancy, educational attainment and standard of living.

> About 79 per cent of Kenya's population lives in rural areas and relies on agriculture for most of its income. Nearly half the country's 40 million people are poor, or unable to meet their daily nutritional requirements. The vast majority of poor people live in rural areas. (IFAD 2009)

Over two-thirds of the population are involved in agriculture in Kenya, growing, herding, and fishing for food that serves a strong domestic demand for national produce. Much has been made of the country's exports of tea, sisal, coffee, sugar, and horticultural products by those primarily interested in GDP growth. But it is the work of the majority – the small, family-run farms in both rural and urban areas – that protects the food sovereignty of Kenya, meeting food needs and providing a living for the bulk of the population while conserving the local environment. Small-scale farmers supply 80 per cent of the food consumed in Kenya's urban areas, and up to 65 per cent of total food production is bartered, exchanged, and consumed within the country – often outside of the formal economy, yet linked strongly to culture and tradition.

Kenya's small-scale food producers face threats which combine periodically to severely undermine food systems and livelihoods. Droughts in 2008, coupled with post-election violence, reduced the country's food supply as farmers, particularly in the Rift Valley, were forced to abandon their crops. Food shortages open the way for greater imports and food dumping, particularly of wheat, rice, maize and sugar products, which undercut local costs of production. Part of the problem is that local farmers, who have been neglected for years by agricultural policies, are

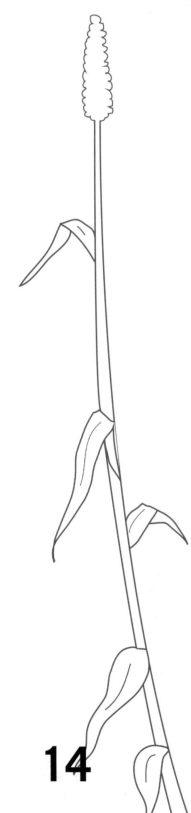

Traditional food networks in Kenya not only share food, but also spread techniques and technologies

now encouraged to produce for export markets, and are pushed towards greater use of fertilisers, pesticides and so-called 'improved' seeds to increase yields and incomes. Yet the history of commercial agriculture in Kenya has benefited the few and put great strains on the natural environment even in the most productive areas. This chapter demonstrates that, despite these pressures, the traditional food networks in Kenya operate well not only for sharing food, but also in spreading techniques and technologies that can help farmers retain their food sovereignty and prosper.

Kenya's production

Smallholder farming takes place across Kenya, with families producing food in ways largely determined by the local conditions of the country's varied climate, topography, and ecology. Only 15–17 per cent of land is classed as fully fertile and receiving good rainfall. These areas, close to the east coast, around the central highlands, and by Lake Victoria in the west, are inhabited by the bulk of the population, yet here the intensive export-driven farms own the largest land areas with the best access to infrastructure (McIntyre et al. 2009). From the highly cramped productive areas, out across the remaining semi-arid and arid lands, smallholder farmers grow crops, artisanal fishers work on the lakes and coastline, and pastoralists roam with herds of livestock. Most food producers with land practise mixed farming of arable production and animal keeping and their farming is determined by local conditions. In contrast to the industrial farms, 89 per cent of farmers own less than 3 ha of land, with 47 per cent living on farms of less than 0.6 ha (Gitu 2006).

The smallholders in Kenya produce enough for their own needs and share and barter among friends and neighbours, a system which has enabled rural communities to be largely self-sufficient since the country's independence in the 1960s. Maize – the most popular staple crop – is grown by nearly all farmers with land, and potatoes and plantain are produced to buffer any deficits in maize product. A household will typically use the seeds that they have saved or acquired locally from neighbours or local seed fairs (See Box 3.2), and this exchange helps to preserve indigenous varieties and foster biodiversity – a lifeline in the Eastern areas where the return to traditional seeds from other parts of the country has provided an alternative crop for use in drought periods. Crops are grown using no (or very little) chemical inputs and the harvests of grain and vegetable are swapped along with meat products between households.

Food is not produced or exchanged in isolation from the social and cultural context of the community, but sits at the heart of a wider network of groups and organisations set up to share support. Most farmers are part of a local social institution – such as self-help groups, women's associations, pensioners clubs, or kinship groups – and these organisations often pool their resources in merry-go-round credit schemes and training sessions (Onduru et al. 2002). Labour is sourced locally when households require extra hands for particular tasks or during busy periods. By meeting their own food and support needs through networks, rural communities overcome some of the 'bottlenecks to food security', which 'include farmers' ability to access food crop research findings, demotivated extension workers, tribal clashes and displacement, illiteracy, and rudimentary farming methods' (Gitu 2006).

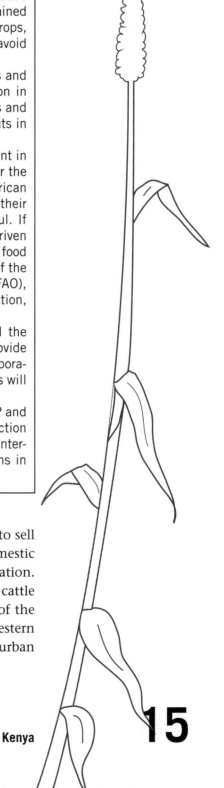

Case study: Strengthening food webs in Embu, Kenya

The Nyaga family is one of about 100 local family farmers in the rural area of Embu. Their food web is mostly satisfied from their own farm's produce, supplemented by purchases using cash from sales of surpluses in the market and through exchanges with neighbours.

The Nyagas grow a variety of food crops in mixed cropping and in rotation, including maize, cabbages, peas and beans, bananas, sugarcane and sweet potatoes, as well as cash crops, including coffee and tea. They also keep different types of livestock – goats, cows, sheep and chickens – to provide meat, milk and eggs for the family and to provide manure for the crops and for soil improvement. Crop diseases on the farm are reduced through rotations.

Limited access to good seeds, appropriate drudgery-reducing technologies and effective extension services makes it harder to improve production; and poor market information reduces potential income. Market demands are changing as richer consumers in the towns are now demanding more meat and fewer vegetables, which may remain unsold; the price offered for the cash crops by traders can also be reduced unexpectedly. Transport to the market is becoming more difficult as poorly maintained tracks and roads become impassable, especially in wet weather. Leftover crops, vegetables and livestock are sometimes sold cheaply at the end of the day to avoid the difficulty of taking them back to the farm on the bad roads and tracks.

The Nyaga family contributes to the food webs of many Embu town residents and could do more if they could be assured of a sale at a fair price. Food provision in this part of Kenya would be strengthened by improvements to extension services and the provision of appropriate inputs, e.g. good quality diverse seeds, improvements in access to Embu town, and better price guarantees.

This is what the Nyaga family hopes might result from the increased investment in agriculture that the Kenyan government is seeking through the agreements under the Comprehensive African Agricultural Development Programme (CAADP) of the African Union, supported by many international donors. But past experience reduces their confidence that the new resources will ever reach them in a way that is helpful. If this were to change and the African Union and international donors were to be driven by the findings of the International Agricultural Assessment (IAASTD), the new food security policy of the European Union, and the agricultural biodiversity policies of the Convention on Biological Diversity and the Food and Agriculture Organization (FAO), all of which favour investment in more ecological practices for local food production, then the Nyaga's future and the local food webs could be secure.

If, however, donors are more driven by the negative policies of AGRA and the World Bank for increased industrial inputs into production systems that provide commodities to an unstable, liberalised market dominated by multinational corporations, then their future is bleak. The food webs in Embu will collapse and farmers will become ensnared in unjust and unfair food chains controlled from afar.

The Nyagas and their representatives in the Kenyan farmers' unions – KENFAP and KSSFF – and their international bodies are calling for more support and protection of their family farming and the local rural-urban food webs. And they look to international movements and organisations to help them give voice to their concerns in relevant national, regional and international forums.

Smallholders' produce is also welcomed nationally. Farmers that are able to sell their surplus on to other markets are the largest contributors to Kenya's domestic food supply, playing an important role in feeding the rest of the population. Subsistence farmers and pastoralists own 90 per cent of the 10 million beef cattle in Kenya. As a result, 80 per cent of milk produced comes from the cattle of the smallholders, mainly in the Rift Valley and the central, eastern, coast and western provinces. Surplus production is collected by traders and taken to markets in urban areas for sale.

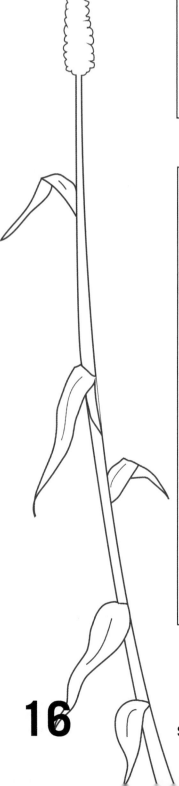

Box 3.1 Kenyan food

Traditional Kenyan food reflects the different cultures of the country's various groups, and most dishes are filling and inexpensive to make. Staple foods consist mainly of corn, maize, potatoes, and beans.

Ugali (a maize-based porridge) and meat are typically eaten together as a dish by those living inland, while households in the eastern coastal areas eat a more varied diet, with African, Arabian, and Indian influences present in their dishes. Fish and coconut-based curries are popular on the coast. The Maasai, cattle-herding groups, eat more simple foods derived to a great extent from the livestock they raise. Cow and goat by-products such as meat and milk provide a high-protein diet for the pastoralists, and they do not eat any wild game or fish. The Kikuyu, Kenya's largest tribe (making up 22% of the population), grow corn, beans, potatoes, and greens around Mount Kenya. These are mashed together to make *irio*, and rolled into balls for dipping into a meat or vegetable stew. In western Kenya, those living near Lake Victoria (the second-largest freshwater lake in the world) prepare many fish stews and vegetable dishes, and rice is a typical accompaniment.

Sukuma wiki is a common dish eaten all over the country, and is made by simmering Kenyan green vegetables with tomatoes. Its name means 'stretch the week' in Swahili as it is a good way of prolonging kitchen supplies. It is typically eaten with *ugali* and sometimes roasted meat or fish. While imports and dumping are becoming more common in Kenya, if people have the money, they prefer to buy domestically produced food, particularly rice and root vegetables, based on their preference for taste, freshness, and nutritional value.

Box 3.2 Seed shows in Tharaka

The partially dry Tharaka district, just east of Mount Kenya, has a poor road network and connection to other areas. During past El Niño rains, the district has been cut off from the rest of the country, leaving farmers to rely largely on their own knowledge and expertise to maintain productive farms. In Maragwa, seed shows are proving a popular way to share agricultural techniques between households.

The annual show is organised around March by the Locational District Committee (LDC) and with support from Practical Action Eastern Africa. Quality traditional seed crops of pearl millet, sorghum, maize, green grams, cowpeas, melons, pumpkins, and pigeon peas are displayed alongside indigenous foods and farming implements. Around the stalls, cultural shows are acted out in which farmers display their seeds, traditional songs and dances promoting seed security and crop diversity. The seed show provides a forum for farmers to share information and exchange seeds within their localities while at the same time exposing them to a wide range of seed varieties from outside the region. It also helps in sharing sound advice about indigenous crop diversity from experienced community seed specialists.

Mrs Kirambia, a farmer interviewed by Practical Action at her seed stall, has participated in every show in Maragwa. Over the years, she has shared and acquired valuable knowledge and seed varieties with fellow farmers. Since coming to the fairs, she has started to grow a variety of *mkombo* (sorghum), which she obtained from a farmer called Peter. The variety originally comes from Sagana, near the Tana River. In 2008, when unreliable rainfall led to a particularly poor harvest, many exhibitors could not attend the seed show that year, as many lacked seeds. But Mrs Kirambia was not affected – she fertilises her farm using cow and goat waste, irrigates her crops with the drip bucket kit she was awarded for coming first in the field day competition, and has learnt the best method for storing her seeds.

Source: Practical Action

Nairobi has many large wholesale markets, including Gikomba, Kibera, Wakulima, Kangemi, and many smaller markets, shops and vendors around the capital. Gikomba market started as an informal place where people could meet and exchange goods; now it is the largest market in Kenya and serves one million people daily – one quarter of the capital's population. It is an extremely busy hub of formal and informal traders, household buyers and hoteliers, passing through from five o'clock in the morning when the market receives its fresh stock. Nearly all food products on sale are produced in Kenya's rural and peri-urban areas, with only one per cent coming from imports or food dumping. Food processing and storage is available for the preparation of fresh produce into saleable items, with butchers and slaughter-houses on site for livestock, and scaling and preparation of fish – mainly Tilapia, from Kisumu – also available.

The popularity of Gikomba and the variety of food vendors occupying it, and other markets, reflects a high demand and preference for domestically produced food. 'Indigenous foodstuffs constitute an important dimension of the informal economy. These foods include vegetables, sweet potatoes, fruits, bananas, cereals, legumes, fish and meat. [...] Some informal markets are well known for specializing in one particular type of food' (Kinyanjui 2010). The outlets themselves are seen as part of the socio-economic context of Kenya. In a survey of consumers in Nairobi, all but the very highest income bracket preferred to shop at traditional outlets because, as well as being cheaper and easier to access, the shops also offered other services, such as credit (See Table 3.1). Out of 40 retailers surveyed, all had given credit and 75 per cent had an average of KSH1280 loaned to four different people (Ayieko et al. 2005).

The movement of food between surplus and deficit areas is a key characteristic of the Kenyan food system, used to diversify food intake and for livelihood income. For example, 'maize is produced primarily in the medium and high potential areas of the Rift Valley Province. It finds its way to distance deficit areas of north eastern, eastern and coast provinces and the urban centres' (Gitu 2006). However, this system does not function perfectly and has contributed to the escalation of famines in the past, as food supplies have stacked up in areas of high-market opportunity and not reached the deficit areas, despite, in some cases, those going hungry having the money to buy food. This 'artificial shortage of food' is exacerbated by 'the combination of lack of information, impassable road network and movement control of grains' (ibid.). The balance between food and sale crops can be difficult for farmers to maintain because of their inequitable position in markets, and

All but the very highest income bracket prefer to shop at traditional outlets

Table 3.1 Where people shop in Nairobi

Outlet type	Any food item	Staples	Dairy	Meat or egg	Fresh produce
	(% of HH purchasing at least one item from this outlet in the last month)				
Large supermarket	28	26	11	5	6
Small supermarket (not a chain)	32	28	5	2	3
Duka (shop)	90	84	63	58	3
Open air market	83	48	0	24	72
Hawker	25	3	17	2	8
Kiosk	66	20	12	16	56
Butcher	97	0	0	87	0

Source: Ayieko et al. 2005

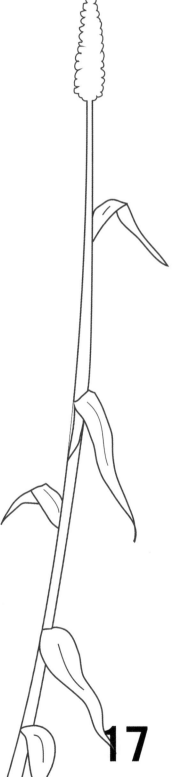

pressure to grow cash crops, meaning some are net maize sellers at harvest time, and net buyers only a few months later (Stephens and Barrett 2010).

Pastoralist networks

Kenya's other great farming group, the nomadic pastoralists making up 25 per cent of the population, lead a far more self-contained food and production system, but are vital for meeting food needs of a large part of the population living outside the most productive zones. Pastoralists travel with their herds of cows, goat, camel, and sheep between grazing and watering points across the vast northern arid and semi-arid areas. Livestock are intrinsically linked to their way of life, and have been for centuries, holding a strong cultural significance prized higher than their economic value. Their frequent travel allows the finely balanced ecology to re-grow and re-charge after use, although the slow onset of climate change is forcing pastoralists to travel further for water and pasture. Prolonged dry spells can seriously diminish their herd.

Pastoralists derive their predominantly meat and milk diet from their livestock, which also provide wool and hair used for making cloth. Before the opening of livestock markets in northern rural areas in the last two decades, exchange in the pastoralist system operated nearly exclusively outside the monetary system. Pastoralists relied solely on trading and bartering in livestock and without use of the Kenyan currency. Groups regularly trade between themselves for more livestock and information, and with the sedentary population for external goods, such as maize. Given the nature of their nomadic lifestyles, their relationships with others have to be dynamic and able to cope with their need to travel in search of pasture. As such, the pastoralist networks are as important for the exchange of information, and must balance 'knowledge of pasture, rainfall, disease, political insecurity and national boundaries with access to markets and infrastructure' (Watson and van Binsbergen 2008). Some pastoralist groups in Africa have developed 'highly sophisticated long-distance trade networks, mak[ing] use of them to pass information about both market conditions and forage resources' (Blench 2001).

The pastoralists' self-contained system is largely in place today, and cattle remain intrinsic to their social as well as economic activity. Yet, since Kenya's first periodic livestock market opened in Samburu district in 1991, they have gradually allowed part of their activity to become integrated into wider markets, and their produce now reaches a larger spectrum of people in Kenya. Groups are increasingly taking their livestock to formal local market points that offer processing, sale and buy opportunities, from which the meat often makes its way to more centralised markets, and eventually the consumer.

The formal market chain for pastoralist produce in the northwest district of Turkana has been mapped (Watson 2008; see Figure 3.1). Pastoralists have most contact with the 12 smaller markets spread throughout the district – such as Oropoi and Lomil in the west, and Kerio in the east, where they take their livestock for slaughter. Goat is the most commonly slaughtered animal, while killing of camel and bulls is reserved for the wealthiest families. The meat is then taken to Turkana's primary markets: Lodwar, Lokichogio and Kakuma, which sit along the main central roadway passing from north to south; and to one market across the border in Uganda. The majority of the produce is sold at these markets where there is a high demand from the local population, and stays within the district, yet just under a third is transported on to the cities of Nairobi, Eldoret, and Kitale, for sale in the markets providing hotels and households.

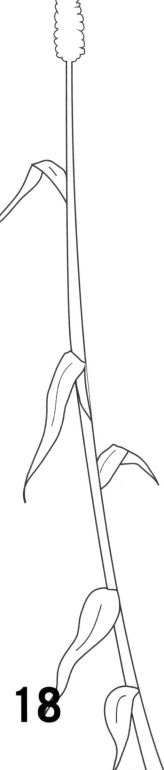

Sustaining local food webs

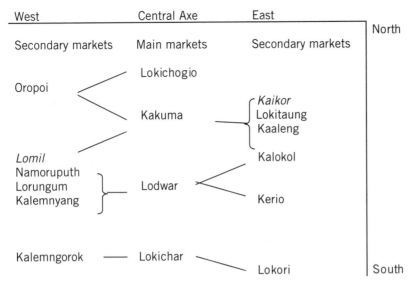

Figure 3.1 Livestock market links in Turkana, Kenya
Source: Watson and van Binsbergen 2008

Pastoralists typically interact with the livestock markets during the dry season, reducing their herd size and providing a monetary income when needed to buy external goods and services, such as veterinary drugs, education for children, and health care. However, they often receive the least reward in the livestock supply chain. The Ministry of Agriculture and the Kenya Meat Commission have withdrawn from the marketing of agricultural commodities, putting the livestock trade in the hands of private traders and informal micro-enterprise (Kibue 2007). In Samburu, neighbouring Turkana, pastoralists face 'a disorganised livestock industry with poor operational capacity, quality standards and unfair trade practices', whilst middlemen and cartels 'benefit from unfair trading and lack of market information' (ibid.). Those involved in the transport of livestock between markets face difficulties with poor road surfaces in many areas, charges from cartels, and the risk of having their cattle raided. Pastoralists are often unable to overcome these problems because of their intermittent use of the physical markets and limited access to market information. Efforts to overcome these issues have begun in Samburu, with the actors in the supply chain – livestock farmers, traders, meat processors and butchers – coming together in a self-help group that promotes price transparency along the market chain, improvements in the hygiene and environment impact of the abattoir at Bahati, and ways to add value to the pastoralists' products.

Building on local networks: Farmer Field Schools

The local networks that foster food production in Kenya – whether at seed fairs, women's groups, or livestock chains – are designed to spread knowledge and skills in order to share food and income opportunities. These networks are now being built upon to enable farmers to tackle the range of threats they face. Over 8000 Kenyan farmers are developing their own solutions through Farmer Field Schools, and participating with other schools in the exchange of their findings. The approach was first developed by FAO in Indonesia in response to rice pests, but it is now used in Kenya and other African countries to deal with a wider range of problems through techniques such as soil productivity improvement, conservation agriculture, control of surface runoff, water harvesting, and improved irrigation. Their model has great importance; a lack of market information and 'modern' technologies are problems frequently cited by agribusinesses and Green Revolution organisations as justifications for pushing more of their products out to greater numbers of farmers.

In Kenya's 283 Farmer Field Schools, men and women meet on their own land at the start of the season to trial and test different methods over the course of a growing season with the support of a facilitator – usually an extension worker or alumni of other farmer schools. The farmers mainly work on solutions to tackle the three most experienced environmental threats to cereal production, namely: the parasitic striga weed, stemborers (moth larvae that eat into maize and sorghum in particular, weakening or killing the plant), and poor soil fertility.

One successful approach trialled and disseminated through the schemes is the Push-Pull technology for crop protection (See Box 3.3). First used in western Kenyan districts around Lake Victoria in 1997, Push-Pull has since been rolled out to eastern Kenya through Farmer Field Schools supported by the Kenya-based International Centre for Insect Physiology and Ecology (ICIPE), NGOs and small businesses. The technology has benefited 40,000 farmers, and yields of maize have increased between by nearly one and 3.5 tonnes per hectare, increasing incomes for nearly 250,000 people in the region (Neondo 2011). Further businesses have been set up by farmers to sell Napier grass and desmodium (ibid.).

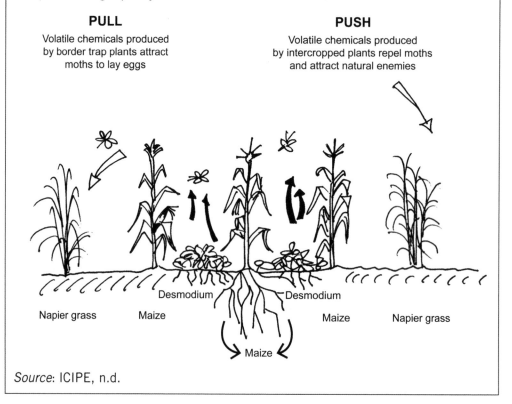

Box 3.3 Push–pull technology

Cereal crops are intercropped with repellent plants such as desmodium, whose fragrances repel the maize stemborer, and bordered by an attractive trap plant, such as Napier grass, which encourages the stemborers to lay eggs in the grass instead of the maize. The Napier grass captures the larvae, and reduces the number that survive to adulthood. Chemicals produced by the roots of the desmodium prevent the striga seeds from attaching to maize roots, killing off the weed and reducing the number of seeds in the soil. Desmodium is a legume plant and improves soil fertility by fixing nitrogen in to the soil. Since both desmodium and Napier are perennial, push–pull technology conserves soil moisture, increases the biodiversity on the farm, and provides high-quality animal fodder (Neondo 2011).

PULL
Volatile chemicals produced by border trap plants attract moths to lay eggs

PUSH
Volatile chemicals produced by intercropped plants repel moths and attract natural enemies

Desmodium   Desmodium

Napier grass   Maize   Maize   Napier grass

Maize

Source: ICIPE, n.d.

The Farmer Field Schools are the main conduit for sharing ecological approaches in Kenya, but, although growing, they are fewer in number compared with the farmer associations focussed and organised around the commodity chain, rather than food systems as a whole or on specific issues. Commercial farming groups are also aping the farmer organisations by acting as collectives and thereby increasing their lobbying power within government. The Farmer Field Schools face issues of sustaining the funding needed to initiate new schools. However, the success of yield increases in Kenya suggest the possibility for schools to become self-financed by the farmer groups themselves (McIntyre et al. 2009). The schools represent value for money, despite the high cost for the activities of the initial farmers; the focus on the sharing between farmers ensures that information and techniques are dispersed and modified widely.

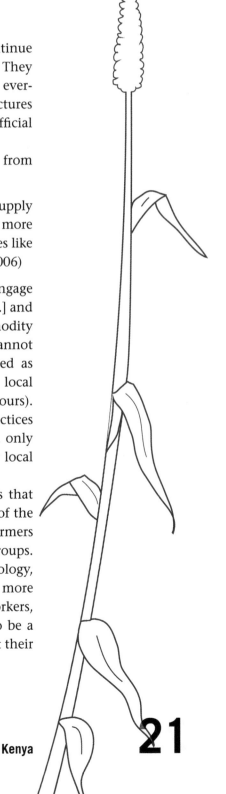

Food insecurity has occurred without any decline in the general supply of food

The future of Kenya's food networks

In the next 10 years, the small-scale farmers and local food webs will continue to play a large, if not greater role, in providing most of the food in Kenya. They have historically provided for most rural households and are now feeding the ever-increasing urban populations too. They are also the only empowering structures for farmers who would otherwise be almost totally marginalised from official attention.

But their efforts currently go unrewarded and do not prevent farmers from falling into hunger for at least part of the year.

In Kenya, food insecurity has occurred without any decline in the general supply of food. In other words, food production per person can increase and yet more people still go hungry. This is basically due to the other intervening variables like food distribution patterns as well as national policies and subsidies. (Gitu 2006)

When hunger is present, proposals to encourage smallholder farmers to engage in global and national 'opportunities for profitable commercial agriculture [...] and intensive farming' are inappropriate (Omiti 2008). The production of commodity goods already puts pressure on farmers to use their land for crops they cannot consume, and the emphasis on the high-value food markets is recognised as diverting food away from places where there is hunger (a perversion that local food webs help to relieve by swapping food between families and neighbours). Furthermore, as Kenyan farmers will increasingly need to adapt their practices and livelihoods with the onset of climate change over the coming decades, only approaches that empower their position to make changes and protect their local ecology can be deemed appropriate.

The existing food webs must be encouraged to flourish and the barriers that prevent them from doing so removed. Support to promote wider exchange of the abundant traditional knowledge in Kenya can be achieved by bringing farmers together at seed fairs, farmer schools, livestock chains and other producer groups. These groups are excellent forums for combining local expertise on the ecology, climate, farming techniques, and markets across regions, and also with more formal information providers, such as research institutions, extension workers, NGOs, and the private sector. Working with farmers has already proved to be a success in Kenya, but only with increased support will they be able to protect their food sovereignty into the future.

4
Mali

An interview with Mamadou Goïta, ROPPA

This chapter is an edited transcript of an interview between Mamadou Goïta, Executive Secretary of the Réseau Des Organisations Paysannes et Producteurs de l'Afrique de l'Ouest (ROPPA), and Patrick Mulvany, Senior Policy Adviser to Practical Action.

Box 4.1 ROPPA

ROPPA is the principal network of peasant organisations and producers in West Africa. It was officially founded in 2000 during a meeting in Cotonou by farmers' organisations from 10 West African countries (Benin, Burkina Faso, the Ivory Coast, Gambia, Guinea, Guinea-Bissau, Mali, Niger, Senegal, and Togo). It is growing and now includes farmers' organisations from other countries in the region.

The network aims to promote and defend the values of sustainable family farming; to inform the members of family farming organisations and agricultural producers' associations about relevant experiences of ROPPA members and the other participants in rural development; to support and to facilitate the consultation and the organisation of small-scale family farmers in all countries in the region and to increase their participation in defining and implementing development policies and programmes in agricultural and rural sectors; and to promote solidarity among peasant organisations worldwide.

Patrick Mulvany: *In recent visits to Ethiopia and Cameroon, I have been reminded how much food is produced locally. I would be interested in your reflections on the strengths and the resilience of these 'local food webs', and how important they are in Mali.*

Mamadou Goïta: In Mali, there are different agroecological systems in the country. If you go in the north you have cattle grazers, pastoralists, and also some farmers on the banks of the River Niger producing local wheat; if you go to the central part of the country, you have regions like Ségou where there are millet and sorghum producers and sometimes maize. This is the area where cotton is produced. If you go to the south to the production area of Sikasso, there are different types of production here, mainly cereals, but also you have staple production, and fruit and so forth. You will find that there is a cultural background to the ways people are producing in these areas.

Despite the fact that there are very aggressive ways of introducing many imported foods – pasta from Italy, which you can have in many cities, and rice from different Asian countries – you find that the production of the people provides the core of the food system. In a typical family – I can talk about Sikasso as this is the area that I am from – you will find that up to 96–97 per cent of the food ingredients consumed are locally produced. I can say now that in Mali, and in Burkina Faso as well, the consumption of local food is growing.

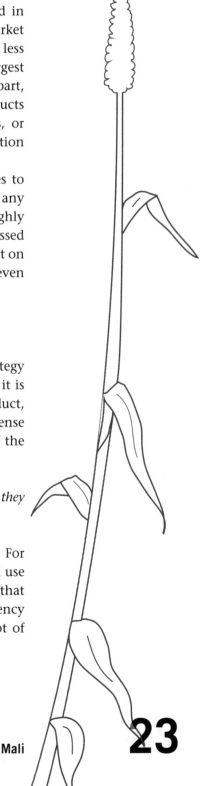

In a typical family, up to 96–97% of the food ingredients consumed are locally produced

What is the portion of food that is in the money market and what is outside?

I can give an idea of what from the farm comes on the markets to be sold in cities. The average proportion of the crop that the farmer will send to the market via small-scale traders, or even the government buying for security stock, is less than 30 per cent. Even accounting for the rice producing areas, where the largest proportion goes to the market, it is still less than 30 per cent. For the most part, farmers are moving between their own consumption and the exchange of products between different regions, cereals for fruits sometimes, or roots, like yams, or potatoes, or sweet potatoes, and to some extent food is exchanged for production equipment. So the system is mainly out of the market system.

For some products, though, such as cotton, 100 per cent of the crop goes to the market because it has been imposed on the country. People do not have any possibility even to retain their crops because of the system itself; cotton is highly dependent on the market, they do not have means to process it, they have accessed credit to produce it, and the company is taking back all of the produce, selling it on the international market and then paying the farmer. The producers do not even know what the system that deals with their cotton once it is sold involves.

Are there any food products that fall into this category?

For this you need to look at some of the products that people call their 'strategy product'. They call it their strategy product in terms of access to money. But it is not a strategy for the country. If you look at sesame, it is a wonderful product, but people are producing mainly for the market. There is a lot to do in this sense because people take up areas of their land for this crop, which is not part of the national food system.

When people are producing for the market, rather than their own consumption, are they tempted to use more chemical inputs?

There is correlation between market orientated products and higher inputs. For their own consumption people won't use pesticides or herbicides, or they will use a small quantity of these, knowing that they are harmful for themselves, and that these inputs will kill the soil, and contribute towards creating more dependency on the international system. But in the areas of Mali where people use a lot of pesticides, they are used on products for the market.

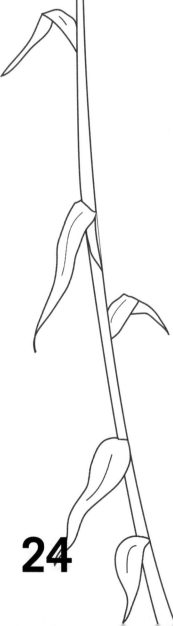

And for the local food webs, in which 70–80 per cent of the food is produced locally, are all the seeds also produced locally?

Yes. For the most-consumed products like millet and sorghum, they use local seeds. The exception is maize now because the most popular variety of maize comes from the research institute.

When you get to a big city, like Bamako, what is the proportion of food that is provided by people from local areas?

I do not have a clear picture of this, but I always say that Mali is self-sufficient in food. There are some people that do not have access to this food for various reasons, and these people are mostly in the cities or in remote regions.

It was common in the past that people would eat imported food, oil and maize from the World Food Programme. But this is disappearing; the only exceptions today are in rice consumption, which has become a problematic thing, and those that are eating pasta. Even with the World Food Programme, we were fighting for them to buy only local food grown in the south of the country for those, especially pastoralists, in the northern and eastern parts of the country, touching on the Sahara, who lack access to cereals.

In the Loi d'Orientation Agricole, Mali's agricultural law, you have been very successful in getting the Malian government to be quite clear about how to defend family farming. Can you briefly describe this?

This was a very interesting process because farmers' groups have been responsible for implementing the consultation process at the local, regional and national level, to write this document, so it has been in consultation with the population. Even though there are some chapters of this law that can be improved, such as the parts referring to the land issue, at least it has been a process led by farmers' associations. We engaged in this process. It took 18 months in total, with farmers' organisations and their allies helping with the methodology so that all Malians can participate in the debate.

The consultation started at the local level to capture the vision of Malian men and women for our agriculture in the coming 50 years; this information was taken to the regional consultations, where we took into consideration the law and debated specific thematic areas that need deeper exploration – I'm talking about fisheries, seed systems, finance for agriculture, rural infrastructure, land issues and more. These are the topics we need to discuss further at the local and regional level. We then ran a national workshop on these seven key areas, as well further ones on agricultural research and marginalised groups – how to develop specific areas for marginalised people – and pastoralism.

How are urban consumers involved and how they will the benefit from the law?

They have been deeply involved. There is a whole chapter on consumers because their participation and point of view has been involved at the local level, and they have also been part of the working groups and the steering committees. There is a whole chapter on how the family farming system has to feed the cities. There is another chapter on processing, and how women are involved in food processing. This was followed by a campaign to raise awareness of how women processors are feeding the cities. As part of this, we realised that there has been an increase by 35 per cent in the amount of food processed in the cities – this is where you will find local products that are easily used by urban populations – and this is increasing the types of local food available.

Why are the poorer people in the cities dependent on purchasing food when the majority of the country gets its food through a local food system without the need for money?

For those without access to the informal food economy, they have to rely on the market and, through use of perverse subsidies, the government favours imported food. For example, in 2010, when there was a cereals surplus, the government gave CFA23 billion to free-traders to import rice for cereal banks which undercut local women's sales. So even though there was a good quantity of produce, they continued to import. When people have income problems and have little to exchange they will seek to save some money by buying at, say, CFA100 some imported food rather than pay CFA110 for the local produce. This is the case for most of the produce in the cities. It is because of the subsidies; otherwise, if it were only in terms of quality, the majority would opt for local produce.

The pressures in Mali to adopt a more industrial food system are significant. Could you summarise who you see as the actors that are trying to undermine food production?

They are hijacking the food system in my country. The first group are those associated with pushing the Green Revolution through Africa. Today, there is a big offensive of this group to change radically the food production system, giving spaces to agro-dealers, those who are selling fertilisers even in the small villages in the remote areas, where they are training people, they are giving them money, and bringing pesticides and herbicides. You know that one of their objectives is to bring these fertilisers to the smallest farmers in the country. This group is made up of foundations, foreign governments, donor agencies, and corporations.

The second group of actors is the bilateral agencies that are doing all this research to argue that we should privatise our agriculture. Just to give you an example – if you look at the case of land-grabbing, this started in 2003 when studies came out on land policies in all West African countries which said that there is too much marginal land in this region, and the best way to use them is to promote foreign investment and privatise the land. They gave the argument that farmers should have security on their land via titles. We know that the title system is killing the food system in different countries because the banks, who used to take your bicycle or your motorbike as guarantee, will never take these items any more knowing that you have titles on your land. The rates of return on the production of cereals are low because cereals are not for the market – they are a socio-economic activity – so many of these farmers will lose their land and sell it to people who have money.

You also have a group of agro-corporations who own many research institutes. In Mali, Cessana is one of the oldest, but also the most well-known, research institute belonging to the National Institute. It is almost 100 per cent funded by an agro-industry company and all the researchers have their salaries paid by the company. The personnel are ex-agro-industrial staff and they have contacts with the industry and its information. The best researchers in our country, and others from Burkina Faso and Niger, are now hired by the agro-industries. For instance with cotton, the researchers are also representatives of the companies promoting cotton in West Africa. So this is to say that this group of corporations, whether they

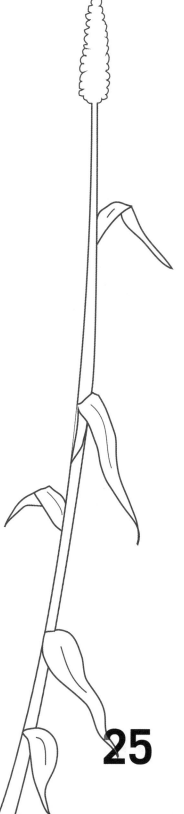

The government favours imported food with the use of perverse subsidies

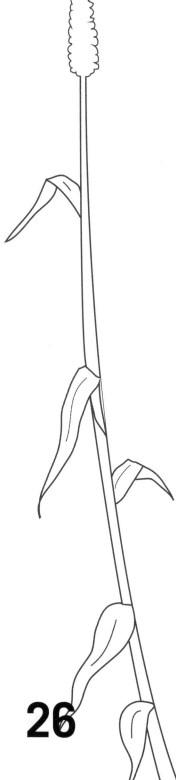

The best researchers in our country, and from Burkina Faso and Niger, are now hired by the agro-industries

are working on seeds or fertilisers, are those that are fighting against the system that is dominated by small-scale farmers using local seed, producing for their own consumption, and giving the surplus to the local market.

Who are the most supportive actors in defending the food system?

It's the farmers' organisations themselves, first. In my region, with ROPPA and the national platform, CNOP, working on family farming systems, just to defend the model of farming, you have these groups on the front line. There are also civil society organisations that understand that they have to help farmers in their fight. But a big majority of international NGOs are defending the position of corporations in Mali and trying to implement projects that are funded by the proponents of the Green Revolution in Africa, who are ready today to push our farming system into the international market. This why they are recruited – to enable access to small-scale farmers who, for them, are resisting against technologies and techniques. Everybody would like to have equipment so they don't have to wake up in the morning at 6 a.m. and go back home at 10 at night. But why are they resisting? Because they know that it is not sustainable and the way these companies want to lead them will take them very far from the original aim of the agricultural system.

Do you think that the combination of these groups that are defending the corporations, the effects of the corporations, and the money which they can use to corrupt the system, is really a danger to the food system in Mali?

It is. We know that family farming is the key point and that the system they want to promote is not sustainable. By now they are very conscious about how to use the international NGOs to push the system they want to see. There is a group of organisations and corporations that are pushing GM crops through international NGOs. This is a problem, and we have to be very, very cautious about what organisations are proposing and who is behind their proposals. The industry's hands are everywhere. We know that most of the international organisations are surviving because of this system; some are resisting, but most are trying to get money from the corporations, and are changing the system by doing so.

What threat do you see to ROPPA and Via Campesina, and to the national members of both platforms, from the new farmer associations that are being set up by industrial interests?

This is really a big fight that is starting now. There is a new mode of hijacking, a kind of sabotage, of what farmers' associations are doing. ROPPA and Vía Campesina have their vision of agriculture; governments also have their associations linked to the Chamber of Agriculture. Now the corporations, via their foundations, are creating their own associations to counteract this. Groups like ROPPA and Vía Campesina have been telling the corporations for so long that Mali, and other African countries, do not want or need their way of marketing agriculture, so the corporations have set up associations to undermine these criticisms. Some states, such as Senegal, are doing the same thing, to destroy the peasant organisation CNCR [Conseil National de Concertation et de coopération des Ruraux] and what family farming has been doing in this country for years. There are also many other small-scale associations set up by international NGOs to weaken the national umbrella organisations, like CNOP [Coordination Nationale des Organisations Paysannes] in Mali. So now threats are coming from all sides.

Given all you've talked about, could you summarise what the priorities for agricultural investments should be?

If you look at all the challenges that agriculture is now facing – I'm talking about land issues, water management, access to equipment that can be used in a sustainable way, using biodiversity but not harming it, climate change, and how to adapt to it – if you look at all these challenges, we realise that they are the result of the fact that the key types of investment that countries are making are not relevant, that the type of investment that international institutions are proposing is not relevant. There is now a big push to invest in agriculture, but the type of investment proposed will not help small-scale farmers, and will completely kill the family farming system.

The best way to invest in agriculture is to first understand the family farming system, as a mode of production, as a mode of consumption, as a mode of life. Then invest in the challenges that the family farming system faces. One big challenge today is to ensure sustainability while increasing production to feed the growing population. This is the challenge, but it is not impossible. As we know, the family farming system has been feeding the population in Mali. I have been doing research on this: except in 2003/04, when we had a pest attack, for every year in the last 12 we have had surplus production. Some parts of the population do not have access to this, because they do not have the income, but this work has been done by the family farming system. Less than one per cent of the production in Mali is from agribusinesses – less than one per cent! This year, we have more than six million tonnes of cereal production. We have been almost doubling production in some crops since the food crisis of 2008. This means there is potential.

The second type of investment is to show farmers that they have security on their land and in their livelihoods. To farm the soils without damaging them, farmers need appropriate tools and better access to water through water management techniques. Local markets also require investment. Knowing that consumers from the cities are more interested in local production, farmers can sell their produce at the local market, instead of international markets where they have no say on prices. Improvements to local markets will convince farmers that there is more reward from feeding our own population. There is already a big trend in people abandoning cotton farming so they can produce food to feed themselves and the population – cotton production has fallen from 620,000 tonnes to less than 180,000 tonnes. Investment should be focussed on how people can manage their land sustainably. This is *not* giving money for fertilisers, which is what is happing today. The money from the Green Revolution organisations is going to what they call 'soil health', which means the use of fertilisers, and what they call 'markets', meaning organising food to go to international markets. They do not touch the essential needs of the family farming systems.

We should be investing in helping people organise their own knowledge on different parts of the production model and promoting the exchange of their knowledge with others, so all can improve their farming systems. Farmers in the north of Mali producing maize, and even rice, have a different system to what people are doing in central Niger. Exchanging the knowledge behind these practices, and the type of the seeds in use, can help each other to improve. In central Mali, we are using what we call an 'integrated system' in a biological fight against crop

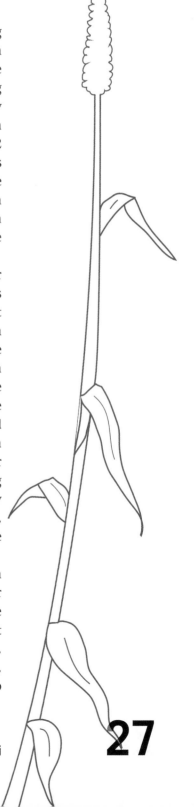

For every year in the last 12, except when we had a pest attack in 2003/04, we have had surplus production

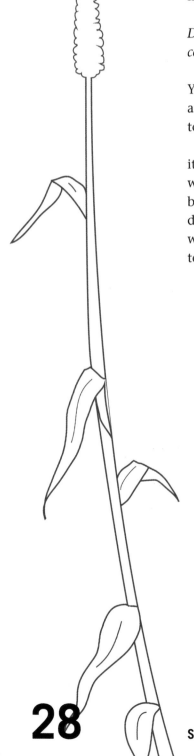

The only way to help Africa develop its agriculture today is to invest in family farming

predators and diseases that affect garden vegetable, millet and sorghum. This system has contributed to improving the yields of some farms by 40–42 per cent – without using any synthetic fertilisers on the farm! We know that, in Niger, those who are using ordinary organic fertilisers, sometimes with only even micro doses of chemical fertiliser, have the best yields in the country. Investment should go to helping in the sharing of these techniques, as well as in the sharing and protection of seeds. This would improve what people are doing. We are already at a level where we can say that things are improving, but I'm sure we can do more.

A final helpful investment would be in promoting the consumption of local produce. This can be done by helping mainly women to process food in a sustainable way. So there is a need for this kind of small-scale agro-industry, which can create jobs at the local level, with equipment that is not too expensive, and can help in feeding the cities. Knowledge sharing, and equipment that can help in a sustainable way, have to be included in the agenda of those who want to invest in agriculture in Mali and Africa as a whole.

Do you believe there is sufficient resilience among small-scale family farmers to be able to continue to feed Africa, while much of the investment is going to systems to destroy them?

Yes, we know if we don't change the trend, if farmer organisations don't wake up and fight against what is going on, and use all we have to change this investment to help small-scale farmers, then they will struggle.

But I know that the trend of resistance today is so strong that no one can stop it. They cannot stop it. Farmer organisations are committed to that. This is why we are so involved in the all the debates surrounding investment, why we have been discussing it today, why we investigate to see where these people will meet to discuss investment – so we can be there to tell them that they are doing things the wrong way, and that the only way to help Africa to develop its agriculture today is to invest in family farming.

5
Conclusion

The local food systems in Africa provide an alternative narrative to the oft-repeated stories about the deficiencies of the continent's agriculture and economy. What is frequently referred to as peasant agriculture or subsistence farming in fact feeds the largest proportion of the populations in Kenya, Cameroon, Mali, and across the continent. Small-scale producers feed those in their local areas, often in exchange for other foods, support, equipment, and labour, and, in doing so, the majority of the population earn a livelihood. In each country, family-run farms are also responding to and catering for the increasing demand for food within Africa's growing urban area, and will become more important as agricultural space decreases in these areas. Furthermore, their production is diverse, and beneficial to their local ecology.

Farmers in each country have their own problems peculiar to their context, yet the local food webs demonstrate the ability to overcome the common state of marginalisation experienced by small-scale farmers. The informal sector in Cameroon has been a long-term reaction to the financial crash and laissez-faire policies of the 1980s. The border markets share food to other areas that have greater food insecurity. Kenya's seed fairs and local merry-go-round schemes help to overcome the geographic isolation faced by many and the general distance from scientific support. As the main food producers within Africa, the support mechanisms within the food networks predominately help women and provide a range of support beyond food production.

Food insecurity in Africa is the result of three decades of failed policies that have cut back public support to agriculture while opening African markets to unfair competition from under-priced, subsidised food products from abroad. Investment in agriculture, drastically reduced, has been oriented towards export crops targeting the global market rather than food crops for domestic consumption. It has promoted the growth of industrial systems that poison the environment and rob land and water from peasants, pastoralists and artisanal fisherfolk. (ROPPA et al. 2011; see Box 5.1)

> Local food webs demonstrate the ability to overcome the marginalisation experienced by small-scale farmers

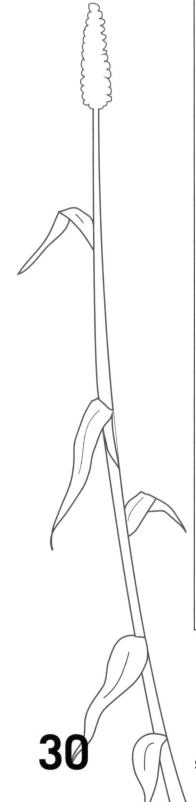

Support is needed to protect African food sovereignty, and the greatest hopes for this lie where governments, organisations, and policy-makers are working with the existing food webs. The Agricultural Law in Mali is a positive example of consultation with food producers to build a system based on their experience and vision, as is the work of ICIPE with farmer field schools to tackle insect pests and striga weed in Kenya using the push-pull technology. These initiatives retain and build on the existing knowledge and expertise held within local food webs.

Box 5.1 Summary Outcomes of the African Farmer Workshop

'Agricultural investment strengthening family farming and sustainable food systems in Africa', 4–5 May 2011, Mfou, Yaoundé, Cameroon

The FO platforms commit to increase their knowledge and strengthen and deepen their analysis of investment dynamics and share information with their members and other networks in PAFO (Pan African Farmers' Organisation). They intend to find ways to increase the capacity of the networks to make the united voices of farmers' organisations heard at all levels, and to defend the interests of all Africa's family farmers, in decision making forums.

They also commit to develop and defend, in different national, regional, continental and international forums, the advocacy strategies which are urgently needed to redirect agricultural investments and defend family farming, sustainable food systems and food sovereignty. The workshop has initiated a process to determine, in different regions, the typology of family farming and its development and support needs and to share this across the continent. The processes of engagement in decision making – nationally, regionally, continentally and internationally – will be promoted especially using the approach adopted by the UN Committee on world Food Security (CFS). In this context the Chair of the Pan African Farmers' Organisation (PAFO) is encouraged to set up a working group to provide information and analysis on key issues concerning agricultural investment, other agricultural policies and related issues.

The farmers' platforms conclude that in order to defend and promote family farming, sustainable food systems and food sovereignty, it is necessary:

1. To realise a common approach in the face of harmful agricultural investments that are capturing productive resources, imposing industrial models of production, and implementing policies, strategies and research and other programmes that undermine local food systems;
2. To redirect agricultural investments towards more agroecological, biodiverse and resilient models of production supported by participatory research, development and extension systems under farmers' control;
3. To give priority to agricultural investments that support the infrastructure and input requirements of sustainable family farming;
4. To secure agricultural investments to improve the effectiveness, capacities and capabilities of farmers' organisations and networks, including their ability of farmers to self-organise, for example in co-operatives that have social, economic, welfare and equity principles;
5. To ensure that there is meaningful participation by our networks and organisations, by using in particular, the approach agreed by States for civil society engagement in the Committee on World Food Security (CFS) which recognises the autonomy of civil society organisations and welcomes them – small-scale food producers in particular – as full participants. Existing arrangements in, for example, the accelerated CAADP and other investment programmes, are not as effective.

Europe has become integrated into a global food system controlled by corporate interests and based on the unsustainable exploitation of resources and people. It is dysfunctional, resulting in increasing obesity in Europe and hunger in other regions; increased social and economic inequity, especially for small-scale food providers and poor consumers; and in environmental degradation. This model of production, also imposed on other regions, drives local farmers off the land, removes small-scale fishers from the seas and confines livestock to factory farms, at home and abroad.

Nyéléni Europe 2012

Compared with the problems that afflict African populations after poor harvests, Europe's food status appears *prima facie* to be functioning well. Food can currently be bought relatively cheaply all year round. Yet the ready availability of food masks problems in the present system; low prices come at the expense of farmers, growers, livestock keepers and fishers, and for the profit of the few dominant retailers and food corporations. In England pig farmers, for example, during the recent price collapse, were losing £3 million a week due to high feed costs and poor prices, while the retailers were reported to be earning large profits from pork products. The difficulties in securing a living are both a cause and effect of the move away from agrarian economies in Europe starting in the early 1800s. Today, the dominance of supermarkets on the high streets of cities, towns, and even the smallest villages reinforces a long drift in food consumer detachment from food producers.

Local food webs in Europe intentionally position themselves as an alternative to this dominant and centralised food industry. They are as much focussed on the consumers as on production. Food producers, outlets, and retailers work closely with campaign groups and community organisations. Though comparatively small compared to the globalised food industry, the local food webs in England, Hungary, and elsewhere have commitment and show creative initiatives for reversing the monopolisation of the food system, encouraging consumer consideration of where food is sourced, and engaging people in the growing of food, the communities that surround it, and the local ecology.

Their intervention is timely: the global food industry that keeps supermarkets well-stocked is depleting natural resources and damaging the environment at the sites of production around the world. The emissions from chemical inputs, intensive production techniques, and long-distance travel produce 30 per cent of all greenhouse gases emissions contributing to climate change, which further undermines the natural environment that agriculture relies on. Those in the local food networks are aware that this is not a sustainable position now, and will not be able to feed the expected increase in global population to 9 billion by 2050. This chapter highlights some aspects of their alternative model for the future.

> The dominance of supermarkets on the high streets of cities, towns, and even the smallest villages reinforces a long drift in consumer detachment from food producers

6 England

London .

In 1998, proposals for the opening of a new large supermarket in a community in Suffolk, East Anglia, led to a research project assessing the local food networks in the area. It highlighted the importance and interdependence of food producers, wholesalers, and outlets to the town of Saxmundham and other towns and villages in the surrounding area. In doing so, the research found that local shops were already providing the food that people wanted and needed, but also that 67 of the 81 local retailers expected to go out of business if a new supermarket was introduced to the area (CPRE 1998). Planning permission for the store was finally refused and the initial research led to a series of reports mapping local food webs – from the small, often family run farms to the greengrocers, farmers' markets, or cafés – in locations across England (see Box 6.1). Each report explores the contribution to the economic, environmental, and social setting of the locality, and the series identifies common threats and opportunities that define the shape of England's local food webs.

This chapter outlines the summaries of the first six mapping projects, from Totnes, Sheffield, Birstall, Hastings, Kenilworth and Knutsford. While only a small representation of the local food webs in England, they document the unique characteristics of a model of food production, supply and sale, often overlooked, and form the pilot stages of a larger research project covering 13 more locations, published in 2012 (CPRE 2012).

The benefits of local food webs

In each area covered by the research, the local food web is powered by a demand for local food and a desire to support local production and trade. The inhabitants in Totnes, South Devon, for example, 'recognise that the strong network of small independent shops and producers in the area provides local jobs, and that the great diversity of shops in the town offers variety and range.' In Birstall, 'the overwhelming majority of shoppers interviewed – over 80 per cent – saw supporting local farmers, producers and retailers as one of the main reasons they either bought or would buy local food.' In fulfilling these demands, a multitude and variety of businesses – from family-run farms to butchers, bakers and greengrocers, as well as numerous delicatessens, pubs, markets, cafés, bars, restaurants and sandwich shops – bring great benefits to their local economies.

It also contributes to an improved local environment. All of the reports identified a number of farms that are practising organic or low chemical input agriculture, and many protect the natural landscape and wildlife in the production of food. Over half the farmers producing for Totnes provided wildlife refuges such as beetle banks, trees and hedgerows and species-rich pasture. The areas surrounding Sheffield are part of a local conservation scheme, the Peak District Environmental Quality Mark (see case study). In Hastings, home to the largest beach-launched fishing fleet in the UK, the fish market at Rock-a-Nore achieved its Marine Stewardship Council certificate, a national award, in 2005 for the sustainability of its sole, mackerel and herring fisheries using wide mesh nets, which do not catch smaller fish that are still growing and breeding. These practices were valued by consumers interviewed. The produce is sold in many local organic shops.

Getting this food to the shops, via processors, involves a significant reduction in 'food miles'. It was beyond the scope of the study to capture the carbon footprint of food produce through a lifecycle analysis; however, the level and distance of transport within the food webs is far lower than the more centralised system of the supermarkets. Mapping of the Totnes region (see Figure 6.1) identified over

160 producers directly supplying a wide range of predominantly fresh (i.e. not processed) produce into the town from within 30 miles, with many located only five to ten miles away. More than 50 per cent of outlets surveyed reported that half to over three-quarters of their produce is locally sourced. The mapping in Knutsford identified over 100 businesses supplying the town with a wide range of produce – eggs, meat, vegetables, fruit, apple juice, and beer, as well as cheese, honey and chutney. Again, the large majority of retailers screened in Knutsford directly source their produce from within a 30 mile radius. In all of the areas, farms that sell directly to the consumer reduce the amount of food that has travelled unnecessarily, whether produced far away, sent outside the area for processing or stored at a regional distribution depot.

The production models found in local food webs are unique in their proximity to the end consumers, and the interaction they encourage between the public, the environment, and the provenance of their food. Community Supported Agriculture (CSA) schemes are running in three of the six food webs (with Sheffield hosting five), attracting a membership of people wanting to buy local produce and willing to contribute to its production. At the Canalside CSA near Kenilworth, over 100 members buy into a share of the organic vegetable harvest, and volunteer to help throughout the year with planting, collecting, construction, teaching, and general maintenance on the farm. The remainder of the harvest goes to local independent food retailers in the nearby towns. As part of its vision, Canalside supports other like-minded projects, hosting visits for groups looking to set up CSAs and mentoring

Picks Farm, Birstall, is a traditional mixed family farm passed down through generations. It is Organic Farmers and Growers Association certified: 'Our ethos is to farm in harmony with nature'. The farm prefers to sell their produce directly to the public in the local area, thus significantly reducing the distance produce has to travel from field to outlet.

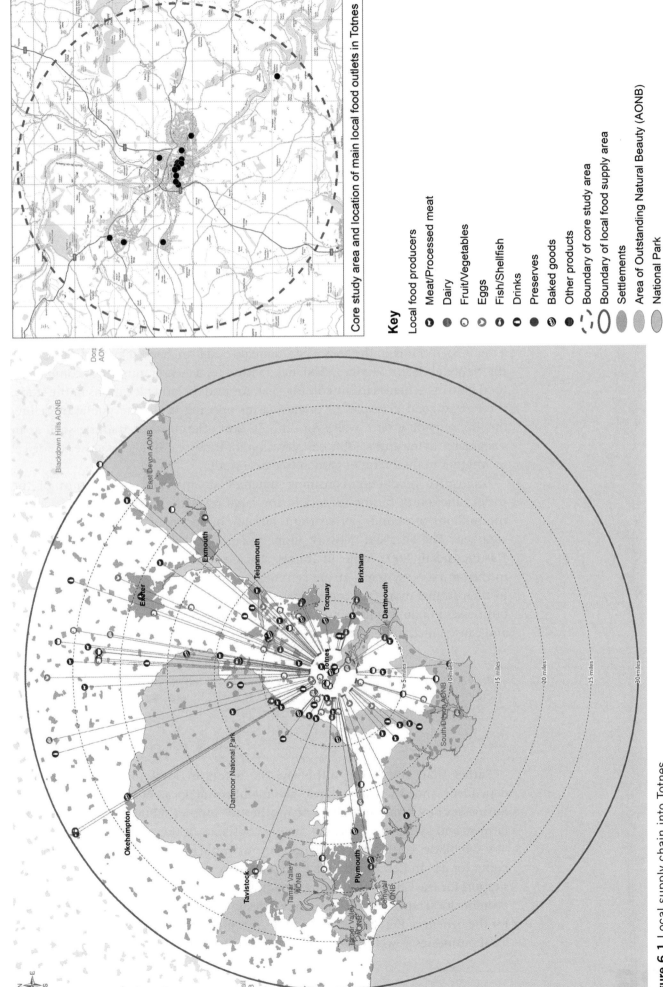

Figure 6.1 Local supply chain into Totnes

Note: contains Ordnance Survey data © Crown copyright and database right 2010

Core study area and location of main local food outlets in Totnes

Key

Local food producers

- Meat/Processed meat
- Dairy
- Fruit/Vegetables
- Eggs
- Fish/Shellfish
- Drinks
- Preserves
- Baked goods
- Other products

Boundary of core study area

Boundary of local food supply area

Settlements

Area of Outstanding Natural Beauty (AONB)

National Park

Rather than competing ruthlessly, the actors in local food webs are interdependent

a new CSA forming in the area. The Sheffield Food Plan, backed by the Council and the National Health Service (NHS), has a vision for a greater number of community food growing schemes in the coming year. Around the other locations in the study, there were good examples of private farms opening up to the public by selling on site, providing farm walks for schools, and offering skills training such as in sustainable living and wildlife conservation for those wanting to practise ecological techniques in their farm or garden (see case study).

Innovative production/consumer schemes are matched by a return of the social function of businesses lost to the large retailers. Local food sales reach in the millions of pounds per year and employ hundreds of people in outlets and suppliers. The Sheffield network supports employment for around 2200 people, Hastings nearly 800 people; in Totnes, a much smaller locality, 1000 people work in the local food system – 10 per cent of the residents in employment. In addition to their formal monetary contribution to the regional economy, nearly all of the businesses in pilot studies across the regions also support an array of local charities and causes, medical services and sports clubs.

> We've been here 10 years and see the town as a big family. Everybody contributes by helping each other. If money is kept within the town, it helps the town grow, especially as Knutsford is located between big cities.
>
> *Retailer, Knutsford*

Rather than competing ruthlessly, the actors in local food webs are interdependent and, in many places, are members of local business communities. Businesses buy from and sell to each other to 'support fellow local tradespeople, farmers and suppliers.' Suppliers too are conscious of this reciprocal relationship: 'It's symbiotic: continuing a relationship with our shops is better for shops and better for us.' In Kenilworth, for example, many refer to their membership of and support for the Chamber of Trade, and praise the town's website as a great tool to promote local businesses. 'There is a real desire for business people to work together for the benefit of Kenilworth as a whole'. A significant number also advertise other local businesses as well as local events in their windows.

36

The sense of community is passed on to the public. Shops and cafés are seen by the customers interviewed in many areas of the study as social hubs, places for people to 'meet up, talk and exchange news and views', and 'talk about their health problems'. Staff are recognised as being helpful and knowledgeable about the products they are selling, and valued for going beyond a standard retail service to lending a 'listening ear to people'. In Sheffield, over half the outlets offer various forms of informal and practical support to their customers, including deliveries to older and disabled customers, help with carrying heavy shopping, and wider support for their welfare. Nearly half of outlets interviewed in Birstall offer some form of delivery, a service replicated across all the food webs, in some instances without charge.

> We have many elderly customers that have been shopping with us for years and they often ask us to bring them things when they cannot get out which we do with pleasure no matter how small the order.
>
> *Shop owner, Sheffield*

Box 6.2 Key Findings from local food web mapping in Sheffield

- Production of local food supports the viability and diversity of farming in the area and helps shape and maintain the character of the local countryside. Over 90 local shops and other food outlets are servicing public demand for locally sourced, fresh, high quality food, and are supported by a short supply chain.
- Local producers supply food directly to outlets in Sheffield from within 30 miles, reducing food miles and related pollution.
- There are several examples of strong community food enterprises which increase access to locally produced fresh food and offer schools, disadvantaged groups and the wider public the opportunity to learn and to engage with food production and the land. Many outlets contribute to their community by offering extra support, particularly to the elderly and disabled; nine in ten support local good causes.
- Local food outlets provide valuable local jobs with potentially over 800 jobs at outlets in the study area and a further 1,400 at local suppliers.
- Local food sales in the area of Sheffield studied amount potentially to £6–16 million per annum.

Challenges and barriers

Ubiquitous across all the food webs surveyed is the competition faced from supermarkets, which influence the ways in which food is produced, distributed, and marketed to consumers throughout England. Each actor in local food webs is affected; farmers, food processing businesses, and the businesses which service them may struggle to compete. In some of the locations studied, infrastructure, such as the availability of small abattoirs and processing plants, has been lost or moved further away, increasing the transport costs for local producers.

Higher costs, and the inability to access the same economies of scale, result in the most apparent difference to consumers between locally produced and marketed food and supermarket produce: higher prices. Despite many consumers expressing that they are willing to pay more for local food, retailers in nearly all areas studied reported that it is hard to stay competitive with supermarkets, particularly when they battle to have the lowest prices. In certain areas of Sheffield where there is a higher level of deprivation, fast food outlets are more prevalent than local or

> In areas with higher levels of deprivation, fast food outlets are more prevalent than local or even fresh food

even fresh food. These areas were found to have a low awareness of and access to local foods despite the range on offer in the city. However, Totnes seems to have generated a commitment to local food across all income ranges, and findings from later research in Burnley, Shrewsbury and Darlington show local markets do cater for a broad section of society.

The marketability of local produce has other problems in reaching wider audiences. In many of the areas, the seasonality of produce puts food providers at a disadvantage to supermarkets, which can stock a wide range of products throughout the year, sourced internationally. In some areas, there is a perceived lack in the availability of local food, and most customers interviewed believed it is often difficult to identify local food in shops because of the absence of clear labelling.

Box 6.3 Recommendations to strengthen the local food web

In order to protect the local food networks, the report series produced a number of suggestions. Some of the recommendations deal with locally specific issues, such as retail development plans in the face of proposals for new supermarkets, but many are relevant across the country.

How local authorities can help

The local food web depends ultimately on local demand. The public sector, including local education authorities, schools and hospitals, can contribute to stimulating demand. They can strongly support small and local producers by developing more sustainable procurement. Public procurement officers can increase opportunities for small local producers by:
- setting specifications for the freshness, seasonality and frequency of delivery of produce;
- strong retail policies to promote retail diversity and control the scale and location of new large scale food stores; and
- splitting larger contracts into lots, for example into product groups or by distribution area.

How businesses can help

Shopper surveys showed that lack of clear labelling prevented people buying more local food. Outlets could highlight local produce by:
- ensuring genuinely local produce is better defined (for example reared, grown, processed within 30 miles) to build shopper confidence;
- establishing a local section in store;
- using on-shelf signs;
- developing a 'local to ...' brand with on-product stickers or signs; and
- using a blackboard to list local, seasonal products and the distance they have travelled.

How the community and individuals can help
- Spread spending across a range of outlets and support those that stock high levels of local food especially your local farm shops.
- If there is no shop nearby selling local produce, seek out a local box scheme (see the local food directory).
- Ask outlets serving food where it comes from and how it is produced: each time you ask it makes businesses think about their buying policy.
- Give shops feedback to help them improve and ask your local supermarket to stock more local lines.
- Contact your local planning authority and local councillors to bring the findings in this report to their attention. Ask them to show strong support for your local food web in their policies, including supporting a farmers' market in your area.

Source: CPRE 2011b

---

7 Hungary

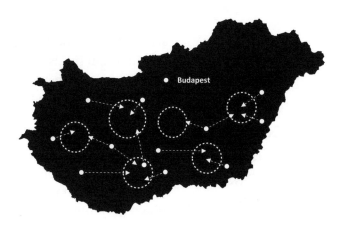

As the country with the most fertile land in the European Union, agriculture has played and continues to play a large role in Hungary's social, economic and cultural history. From the land reform in 1945, small, family-owned farms flourished, sharing confiscated agricultural equipment as communal property, and increasing national production by 50 per cent in three years through their hard work. Soviet rule until the end of the 1980s collectivised agricultural production, and diminished the control peasant farmers held over their land by force and imprisonment. During the move to a free-market economy in the 1990s, the country's farmers retained their collective spirit, social cohesion, and knowledge of environmental care, some of the few positive factors of Soviet rule. Today, Hungary still has many laws protecting family-run farms, yet the environmental and social impact of the multinational agribusinesses which have emerged since economic liberalisation is causing concern about the sustainability of the country's food supply. To counteract this, many farmers and organisations are rallying round to protect the local food networks, and re-demonstrating the alternative models to food production.

The Galga Farm Cooperative

Building on the vision of the Gaia Foundation, 15 farms in the Galga Valley region, 40 miles from Budapest, set up an association for the sustainable production of organic produce (see Box 7.1). For two decades, the Galga Farm Cooperative has followed a Community Ecological Governance approach for a holistic under-standing of living systems. The farms are run by concentrating on the community's relationships with their ecosystem, and by passing on information about the local environment to others.

The farming cooperative produces and promotes a range of vegetable, grain, meat and dairy foods without the use of chemical fertilisers or pesticides. Technologies, such as a stone mill, a small-scale milk processor, and a cannery, are used to reduce drudgery, not to do away with labour – Galga Farm follows in the tradition of

Hungary's 'Ant' cooperatives, whose name refers to the productivity of the insects achieved by working communally. The produce from the farm easily meets the consumption needs of the members, and surpluses are sold at the local market.

In keeping with the original educational work of the Gaia Foundation, Galga Farm members run courses and on-site visits on the organic and sustainable agricultural practised on the farm, which have encouraged non-member farmers in the region to produce in more environmentally beneficial ways. The Farm Cooperative teaches between 180 and 250 children and adults each year. The valley, an area of the 28 towns and villages with a population of 180,000, now has its own marketing cooperative made up of Galga Farm members and neighbouring farms, which promotes the organic produce from the Galga region, and has connected into a nation-wide Hungarian Federation of Marketing Cooperatives. Furthermore, the Gaia Foundation has led a participatory planning process to formulate a rural development plan for the Galga Valley region. A flagship project of this is the recent construction of an eco-village, in which fifty households not only farm organically, but generate their energy from renewable sources and utilise the compost potential from their waste disposal.

Box 7.1 Galga Farm Cooperative

The Galga Farm Cooperative works along the following principles in order to produce organic food that sustains the local ecology:
1. Voluntary and open membership
2. Democratic member control
3. Member economic participation
4. Autonomy and independence
5. Education, training and information
6. Cooperation among cooperatives
7. Concern for community

The farmers' market on Hunyadi square and The Market: Our Treasure citizens' group

Since the 1890s, the Hunyadi market in downtown Budapest functioned as an indoor market hall, and was joined by an outdoor farmers' market in the 1950s. It is described as the neighbourhood's 'pantry', offering fresh and affordable food from the region – fruit, vegetables, jams, preserves and meats – to the neighbourhood's inhabitants. The outdoor market section gives space to 75 contracted small-scale farmers, mostly from settlements within a 100 km radius of Budapest. Nearly all rely on the market as their main income source, while others carry out agricultural work as a secondary activity, including retired persons who maintain small farms.

Recent threats to the market and the small-scale farmers' livelihoods have galvanised a community resistance around Hunyadi. The district's plans to construct an underground garage underneath the outdoor market, and allow the opening of supermarkets within the market hall, resulted in a flawed and corrupted urban 'modernisation' project. This raised indignation among local inhabitants, who created a citizens' group entitled The Market: Our Treasure in the summer of 2007 to defend the market. Retaining local access to quality food on the farmers' market became a symbolic fight for the inner city's last outdoor market, and a practical battle for ensuring the availability of fresh and affordable food in the area.

The citizens' group works on a voluntary basis. Their campaign's first phase focussed mainly on legal work, understanding the mechanism behind tendering procedures, and technical urban planning questions. An important issue concerned the mobilisation of farmers and a larger pool of inhabitants from the neighbourhoods and other sympathisers, including the collection of signatures for petitions on different issues. Following the project's disclosure, the local authorities moved to a consensus on the necessity to maintain the outdoor market, while 'modernising and renewing' it. The project has now moved to a different phase involving discussions on how the outdoor market can be improved and made attractive. Throughout these activities, the citizens' group maintains a blog to promote quality food, local democracy and the reclaiming of public spaces.

Impact of public policies

The Hunyadi market revealed that there is a significant problem in ensuring the transparency of tendering procedures at the level of local authorities. Combined with the lack of any consultation process with local communities, this can lead to decisions taken by local authorities that do not correspond to the needs and priorities of their local constituencies. With EU accession, new funds are available for carrying out participatory processes in urban planning. However, the lack of competence and understanding of local authorities and other professionals entrusted with implementing these processes results in superficial and inefficient consultations, which do not achieve their original aims.

Another problem is that the current regulation on markets and fairs does not allow farmers to be clearly distinguished from traders and other types of vendors, so consumers do not know, and can have no guarantee, about the origins of the products purchased, unless they know the farmer personally. In the same vein, farmers sometimes receive contradictory and confusing information from the authorities supervising local markets about the types of products they are entitled to sell.

Success strategies

The creation of an informal citizens' group that strengthened the existing links and communication between farmers, residents in the local neighbourhood, and local authorities was the first step to success of this alternative food network.

The participation of these actors was crucial for investigating and examining the urban planning projects of local authorities.

The group provides a democratic, non-hierarchical space with the capacity to mobilise a pool of resourceful people and experts. This has been crucial in the success of the campaign for saving the market. Those offering their services have included volunteers helping out in collecting signatures, distributing fliers and putting up posters; legal experts helping with lawsuits; forestry experts evaluating the state of trees in the park next to the outdoor market; architects; and guerrilla clowns mobilizing public opinion in a creative way.

Future survival and expansion

As renewal and revitalisation of the market gets under way, an important goal is to ensure that the local authorities in charge consider the needs of small-scale farmers and consumers, as well as citizens living in the neighbourhood. The objectives are to increase the number of stalls available for small-scale farmers, attract new farmers, and ensure that the rental fees for stalls remain affordable. Making better use of the market space by introducing afternoon and evening markets, and organising thematic gastronomic festivals and cultural programmes are also key actions planned for attracting more consumers and mobilising inhabitants from the neighbourhood.

Farmers within the group plan to widen their product range and improve quality by seeking training and advice on alternative farming methods (e.g. permaculture), introducing more local fruits and vegetable varieties as well as curiosities (e.g. okra, coriander, forgotten or edible wild plants), and ways to process their products.

The campaign strategy – which originally focussed on problems linked to urban planning issues – has now been widened to include plans to increase the awareness around the values and benefits of the farmers' market. The citizens' group plans to publish information on products found on the market, recipes, food or farmers' portraits, and eventually to organise trips to local farms and cooking activities for the market's customers. To do this, raising funds will be necessary, as a significant amount of work is currently carried out on an unpaid, voluntary basis.

Alliance for the Living Tisza (SZÖVET)

Since its creation in 2006, SZÖVET has worked to improve the living conditions of communities along the Tisza River, in north-eastern Hungary – an area characterised by a poor economic situation and high unemployment rates – and to ensure the safety of the local population against flooding. The alliance is made up of 30 small-scale farmers from the region, local service providers, some supportive local municipalities, and researchers. Its agenda of sustainable landscape management and economic regeneration entails supporting sustainable small-scale family farming, fostering co-operation between farmers and communities, and preserving and promoting the region's ecological values, which include a range of local fruit tree varieties, mainly preserved in old orchards and forests.

The organisation's direct marketing activities developed significantly in 2008 when supermarkets provoked the 'cherry and apple scandals' by pushing prices below production costs. An unprecedented wave of farmers' protests spread countrywide. In an act of solidarity, SZÖVET organised 'cherry saving actions', buying the sour cherries from those farmers that were unable to sell at the low prices to the supermarkets and selling them directly to customers at Budapest's farmer markets. Their actions were a huge success – 16 tonnes of cherries were sold and the region experienced a large inflow of conscious consumers attracted by local products and committed to standing up for farmers during the crisis. Encouraged by this, SZÖVET began to organise regular direct marketing activities with a wider range of farmers' produce.

Today, the Alliance for the Living Tisza operates on a weekly basis on four farmers' markets in Budapest, integrating pre-ordering and home delivery to its services. In addition, it started to develop partnerships with shops in Budapest which now sell its processed products (juices and jams). The Alliance began to promote local agro-tourism activities to attract new customers to the regions and encourage them to discover its ecological and cultural values. In a decisive move, SZÖVET developed the 'Living Tisza' certification label for farmers and service providers in the region to add value to products of special provenance and produced using ecologically sustainable farming methods. In 2008, SZÖVET also began legal work to clarify the regulatory obstacles impeding the development of direct marketing.

Impact of public policies

SZÖVET identified the smallholder decree (14/2006, II.16) as an important obstacle to developing and expanding direct marketing initiatives. The decree regulates food production, processing and marketing by small-scale family farmers, and was adopted in 2006 by the Ministry of Agriculture jointly with the Ministries of Health as well as the Ministry of Social Affairs and Employment. The decree poses unreasonable quantitative and hygienic restrictions on certain product categories such as fresh meat, processed vegetable and fruit products. The slaughter of goats, pigs, sheep, and cattle must take place in officially recognised facilities. However, many local and national abattoirs closed down after EU accession, leaving large areas without adequate facilities for small-scale meat production. Another problematic area is the ban on the marketing of processed products in shops and restaurants, while fresh milk produced by small farmers is also excluded from public procurement programmes (for schools and hospitals, etc.).

Civil society organisations, including the Alliance for the Living Tisza and Védegylet, launched a lobbying campaign in 2009. Their demand is that the Ministry of Agriculture modifies the decree by taking full advantage of the derogations on the continued use of traditional methods at any of the stages of production, processing or distribution of food specified by the European Commission (EC) regulation on the hygiene of foodstuffs (852/2004).

Food processing and direct marketing by small farmers are also influenced by decrees governing markets and fairs and by diverse food hygiene regulations, which do not fall under the jurisdiction of the Ministry of Agriculture. The lack of coordination between these ministries means that the legal environment of small producers is rarely updated simultaneously and businesses face an inconsistent legal framework.

Success strategies

The development of partnerships with local processing facilities, the organisation of logistics linked to marketing (transport, storage), and the diversification of marketing channels, including farmers' markets, shops and agro-tourism, have been key in ensuring the initiative's economic viability.

Introducing the 'Living Tisza' label has been another important strategy for gaining added value by emphasizing the local origin of products and environmentally sustainable farming methods. This flexible certification scheme is well adapted to the needs of small farmers in Hungary. It is also inexpensive and entails minimal administration, while empowering farmers by allowing them to select from optional product features linked to the label, thereby taking personal responsibility for guaranteeing product quality. Special care in using the label – farmers must clearly state their products' origins and quality – and responding to consumers' questions play a large part in developing relationships and trust between producers and consumers.

The Alliance's capacity to pool and share resources – from community activists who mobilise consumers through e-mail lists for direct selling opportunities, to legal experts working on the smallholder decree – making it well-placed for mobilisation has also constituted a key factor in successfully dealing with the complexity of issues facing Tisza food producers.

> The decree poses unreasonable quantitative and hygienic restrictions on certain product categories

Future survival and expansion

The Alliance's future plans include raising funds for building its own processing facilities and additional storage space near farmers' markets and other direct marketing venues in the region. SZÖVET also hopes to attract more farmers and service providers interested in joining the 'Living Tisza' label. Lobbying to ease the rules on food processing and direct marketing by small-scale family farmers is a further priority.

8 Conclusion

The European local food networks have a hint of protest running through them. Many involved find common cause in protecting and utilising existing skills, the local environment, and the culinary heritage of their locality.

In the farmers' protests in Hungary, and smallholder farmers' struggles in England, many are realising that supplying direct to consumers is a way to sustain their income, rather than be subject to the vagaries of supermarkets. Consumers, too, are increasingly realising that supermarkets, and the industrial production on which they depend, are not the only way to source food, and better options are available within their community that benefit the environment and local economy. The examples in this book show that there is an understanding, even from those that predominately shop in supermarkets, that supporting local food networks is important. The success in Hungary has shown consumers that where they spend their money is a powerful act. Buying direct from a farmer or from local suppliers connects consumers keen to know more about the provenance of their food with farmers who can achieve greater control over their market. Some of the initiatives around community supported agriculture provide a viable alternative economic model for supplying food.

The resurgence in demand for local food combines with environmental and social concerns about how food is produced and how far it has travelled. The success of local food movements in creating communities, such as the Community Supported Agriculture schemes, and at Galga Farm in Hungary, is dependent on support from consumers who may, additionally, be prepared to contribute labour and skills to local enterprises.

In Africa, locally produced food is the norm in most countries, with most of it produced without chemical inputs. Locally produced organic food in Europe is breaking out of the 'lifestyle choice' niche and coming to be a greater part of people's normal food. There is still a long way to go. As supermarkets compete in their 'race to the bottom' (i.e. to be the cheapest), it may be harder for small-scale food producers and other actors in a local food web to 'win'. Education about the benefits of local food production and addressing misconceptions over the perceived higher 'costs' of this food will have to be combined with greater local, national, and regional support in defending and maintaining local food provision.

Table 8.1 Policies which may help or hinder local food systems in Austria, England, France, Hungary, and Poland

Policy	Hindering (or not helping)	Facilitating
CAP pillar 1 basis for payments	Historic basis reinforces earlier drive for productivity (AT, FR)	Area basis opens up broader options, especially for new entrants to farming (HU, PL, EN – which has its own CAP rules).
CAP pillar 2 (Rural Development Programme, including Leader)	'Modernisation' and efficiency measures for standard agri-products to compete better in distant markets (all five countries) Environmental protection mainly beyond agriculture, e.g. by withdrawing less productive farmland (all) Each grant or investment has a high minimum level (and/or a co-funding requirement), thus benefiting large processors	Leader programmes facilitate cooperative networks among producers and with retailers. Infrastructure for local processing and marketing (AT, England), e.g. for specialty branded products (FR, PL Lower Vistula) Agri-food-tourism links (AT, EN, FR) Agri-ecological cultivation methods, e.g. low-input, organic conversion (EN, FR, PL) Environmental protection via extensification of agricultural methods Small grants are available (EN)
Hygiene regulations	Strict rules presume industrial contexts and methods. For example, government inspectors must be present whenever animals are killed (EN)	Flexibility in rules according to production method and sales context
Hygiene regulations: exemptions for small quantities of primary products in direct sales	Exemptions are narrowly defined – or remain ambiguous and so in a legal 'grey' zone (AT) 'Direct sales' exclude collective marketing (FR) and exclude processed products, both of plant and animal origin, sold to shops or institutions (HU)	Exemptions or lighter rules are broadly, clearly defined (rare) Lighter rules for direct marketing of some primary products (AT) Lighter rules for individual merchants – but not for collective sales (FR)
Hygiene regulations: lighter rules for traditional products	No lighter rules – or even no permission – for some traditional methods (PL) No lighter rules for many animal products (AT)	Exemption for speciality products (PL) Lighter rules for on-farm processing Flexibility for small, marginal, local products derived from crops (EN)
Trading laws	Inconsistent criteria across various laws (all) Invoices are required for every sale (HU) Collective-marketing income counts as profit and so imposes greater tax burdens on producers (FR) No exemptions for small business (EN) No tax benefits linked to certain types of agro-tourism activities (HU)	Direct sales have lighter rules and lower tax (PL) Farm activity and employment have some exemptions from tax (FR) Box schemes are exempt from rules on labelling specific products (EN) Tax benefits for 'primary' producers below a certain annual income receive tax benefits (HU)
Public procurement	'Economically advantageous' criteria favouring the lowest price and larger producers 'Best value' through aggregated purchasing to minimise the price, without clear criteria to justify a higher price (EN) Diet improvement emphasises nutritional and safety criteria (EN, FR)	'Economically advantageous' criteria justifying a higher price – e.g., for quality, freshness, life-cycle analysis, economic development, etc. Contracts are split up by locality and product to favour local suppliers (Cumbria, EN) Diet improvement emphasises quality, e.g. freshly harvested or organic food (AT), but organic can mean more imports rather than local sources
Territorial branding	PDO or PGIs to be marketed anywhere, by-passing local economies Label includes large-scale industrial processors (Warmia Region, PL)	Brands promoting a general territorial identity of food and economic development Label promotes small-scale, quality production with Leader funds (Lower Vistula, PL)

Note: Austria (AT), England (EN), France (FR), Hungary (HU), and Poland (PL).
PDO: Protected Designation of Origin, PGI: Protected Geographical Indication (EU schemes)
Source: FAAN 2010, based on Levidow 2009

9
Common threads

Pouring money into agriculture will not be sufficient; what is most important is to take steps that facilitate the transition towards a low-carbon, resource-preserving type of agriculture that benefits the poorest farmers. This will not happen by chance. It can only happen by design, through strategies and programmes backed by strong political will, and informed by a right-to-food approach.

De Schutter 2011

The common discourse surrounding global food supply has been that Europe and other affluent regions have managed to overcome needless hunger through industrialisation and that Africa needs to emulate this, even though the evidence shows the industrialised system to be unsustainable. The cracks in this narrative, however, are now well open, and it is apparent even to defenders of the industrial food system that the current model will not be adequate for the future.

The local food systems in Africa and Europe are an alternative model to this. Cameroon's *buyam-sellams*, the Community Supported Agriculture schemes in England, and local food networks in Hungary all help ensure that the local economy is strengthened, good food is provided and far less fossil fuel products are used, reducing volatility to oil prices and reducing carbon emissions.

By serving their local areas first, each small-scale food provider presents a counter-balance to the reach of the global food industry. In each country presented here, and many more around the world, these actions manifest into campaigns and resistance movements, not with parochial concerns, but with an understanding of how their situation fits into wider challenges of eradicating hunger, protecting the environment, and reducing the gap between the rich and the poor. Those within the food webs realise the value of food in addressing these issues. They are calling not only for a reorientation of agricultural values and practices, but demonstrating that their model is productive, fair, beneficial, and essential. When the production, processing, and consumption can be supported at a local level, the rewards are as follows:

Economic benefits for the local area. By retaining the whole process of food production within the local area, a greater number of actors are involved and economic reward portioned out across the supply chain. Money earned is put back into the local area, with improvements for businesses and facilities locally. Local food webs are smaller economic systems with greater familiarity and understanding between different actors. In Europe, this leads to a determination to 'buy local' amongst businesses and consumers, whereas in Africa, the informal food systems operate using trust. In Kenya, the support structures, such as the financial merry-go-round schemes, as with the cooperatives in Hungary, are evidence of an alternative financial imperative that prioritises collective progress over hard competition.

Greater conservation of local ecology, and wider environmental benefits. Food producers and consumers have greater responsibility for the natural surroundings as they rely upon them for the sustainability of their livelihood and food supply. Unlike the export producers, who may move locations once an area is degraded and unproductive, it is a lot harder for small, family-run farms to do this, and abandoning the family farm may mean moving to an urban area and out of an agricultural livelihood. Pastoralist groups have shown great perseverance and application of generational knowledge to continue to farm in Kenya's arid and semi-arid areas rather than move to the already overcrowded productive areas. Local organisations and businesses in England and Hungary have created labelling initiatives to preserve the natural environment and beauty of their areas.

Local control over food quality, quantity and supply. Local control over food supply allows for protection of the food web and catalyses new initiatives. The examples from Hungary demonstrate the ability and the power of local-decision making to protect farming livelihoods and the environment, while at the same time creating new schemes to renovate markets, engaging new and existing consumers, and living sustainably. In Cameroon, female entrepreneurs took control of the food supply when national production fell and have managed to create a functioning informal economy that provides nutrition for those beyond their locality in urban areas.

Preservation of relevant knowledge and expertise. Knowledge is used at each level of the food web; from the best ways of working with local soils, geology, weather patterns, seeds and plant life, to the preferences of customers. As shown in the Farmer Field Schools in Kenya, this knowledge can be built upon with farmers to overcome challenges rather than imposing top down solutions. Where farmers do not have knowledge of how their produce is marketed, as with cotton farmers in Mali, this reduces their control of their land and makes them reliant on the pricing of buyers.

Reduced reliance on, or vulnerability to, outside factors. The accumulation of the above factors leads to food systems that can reliably feed the local area, and wider populations, with nutritious food. As such, the justification for food dumping in developing countries is removed, and reliance on supermarkets is reduced in both developed and developing countries. Production with fewer external chemical inputs and with less fossil fuel use reduces vulnerability to oil price fluctuation.

The value and strength of local food webs is that they continue, in the face of pressures from the globalising food system, to feed the majority of the population while preserving the environment. They have endured by developing support and information services throughout the food web despite decades of underinvestment. They have proved their viability and hence deserve greater support and recognition from governments.

Export producers may move locations once an area is degraded and unproductive

Such support for small-scale food providers would contribute towards fulfilling the right to food that is denied to one billion people globally. It would also reduce degradation of natural resources, allowing for more productive agriculture and enabling people to better adapt to climate change, while also reducing the greenhouse gases emissions that contribute to climate change. Within Europe, greater support for local production would improve the resilience of local economies and communities. Supporting what is already being done in both Africa and Europe to meet local food needs for the long term, rather than supporting what currently provides the best short-term returns to government revenues, would provide a more sustainable food system. Local food webs are a cornerstone for the model of food provision that should be prioritised in order to secure our future food.

Food webs have proved their viability and hence deserve greater support and recognition

Annex 1

Other local food schemes in the UK

Making Local Food Work
Making Local Food Work helps people to take ownership of their food and where it comes from by providing advice and support to community food enterprises across England. Making Local Food Work helps community food enterprises across England with some of the challenging aspects of running a business. They have a team of expert mentors and specialists to help local food projects with a range of issues, including developing a business plan and marketing strategy, putting in place a legal structure and governance arrangement, and ensuring compliance with the latest legislation.
www.makinglocalfoodwork.co.uk

Nourish, Scotland's Sustainable Local Food Network
Nourish is a movement of individuals and groups working towards a sustainable Scotland in which in every region people produce more of what they eat and eat more of what they produce. They believe a more localised food system would be better for the environment, health, community and economy of the country, and are creating a food system which is locally based, with shorter supply chains; promotes and respects seasonality; is resilient; is fair and accessible to all; and creates and maintains a sustainable livelihood for producers.
www.nourishscotland.org

FoodMapper
FoodMapper is an innovative digital mapping tool which is used to map all the community growing spaces in Somerset. Users add their knowledge of local allotments, community gardens, and school growing projects as well as initiatives such as food cooperatives, local food retail outlets and markets. Demand for land can also be plotted and an open source base layer aids mapping and the search for access to land, showing farm names and locations of schools and churches and other publicly owned land that could be used as a growing patch. Local food producers can also be mapped.
www.foodmapper.org.uk

Bristol Food Network
The Bristol Food Network aims to link people and groups working on local food issues in the Bristol area. Forum for the Future are currently applying for Lottery funding on behalf of the Network to enable this work to develop, supported by Bristol City Council, the Green Capital Momentum Group and the Health Service. The Bristol Food Network includes several hundred professionals, volunteers, groups and projects working on local food issues in this area, who subscribe to the Bristol Local Food update newsletter.
www.bristol.gov.uk/page/food-bristol

Annex 2

PROPAC

ROPPA

EASTERN AFRICA FARMERS FEDERATION
E A F F
Voice of all farmers in Eastern Africa

African farmer workshop

"Agricultural Investment strengthening family farming and sustainable food systems in Africa"

4 and 5 May 2011, Mfou, Yaoundé, Cameroun

Synthesis Report

This report is dedicated to Ndiogou Fall, founder-president of ROPPA and co-organizer of the Mfou, Yaoundé workshop, who devoted his life to the African peasant movement.

Agricultural Investment strengthening family farming and sustainable food systems in Africa

African Farmer Perspective

The issue of agricultural investment is a key one in Africa and how and where these investments are directed is of considerable concern to African family farmers and their organisations. From CAADP to the reformed Committee on World Food Security, enhanced investment for food security is at the top of the agenda. Although there is now a commitment on the part of multilateral institutions and of a number of donors to give greater priority to supporting family farmers, a number of questions need to be explored in depth in order to ensure that the support proposed is what is wanted by, and is potentially beneficial to, Africa's family farmers and their sustainable food systems. These productive and resilient family farming systems currently provide food for more than 80% of the African population and could deliver more.

The African regional farmers' platforms conclude that in order to defend and promote family farming, sustainable food systems and food sovereignty, it is necessary:

1. to realise a common approach in the face of harmful agricultural investments that are capturing productive resources, imposing industrial models of production, and implementing policies, strategies and research and other programmes that undermine local food systems;

2. to redirect agricultural investments towards more agroecological, biodiverse and resilient models of production supported by participatory research, development and extension systems under farmers' control;

3. to give priority to agricultural investments that support the infrastructure and input requirements of sustainable family farming;

4. to secure agricultural investments to improve the effectiveness, capacities and capabilities of farmers' organisations and networks, including their ability of farmers to self organize, for example in co-operatives that have social, economic, welfare and equity principles;

5. to ensure that there is meaningful participation by our networks and organisations, by using in particular, the approach agreed by States for civil society engagement in the Committee on World Food Security (CFS) which recognizes the autonomy of civil society organizations and welcomes them – small-scale food producers, in particular – as full participants. Existing arrangements in, for example, the accelerated CAADP and other investment programmes, are not as effective.

**African farmer workshop
"Agricultural Investment strengthening family farming and
sustainable food systems in Africa"**

4 and 5 May 2011, Mfou, Yaoundé, Cameroun

1. Introduction

The workshop was organised by PROPAC with ROPPA, EAFF and PAFO. The participants were leaders or staff members of these West, Central and East African regional and continental family farmers' platforms, advisers and representatives of the NGOs in the EuropAfrica network. It was held in Mfou, Cameroun with the support of Terra Nuova, the More and Better network, Concord, Practical Action and FAO.

The issue of agricultural investment is a key one in Africa and how and where these investments are directed is of considerable concern to African family farmers and their organisations. From CAADP to the reformed Committee on World Food Security, enhanced investment for food security is at the top of the agenda. Although there is now a commitment on the part of multilateral institutions and of a number of donors to give greater priority to supporting family farmers, a number of questions need to be explored in depth in order to ensure that the support proposed is what is wanted by, and is potentially beneficial to, Africa's family farmers and their sustainable food systems.

The workshop was designed to start a process of reflection during 2011 that would sharpen and deepen the strategies and methodologies by which the national, regional and continental organisations of family farmers and other small-scale producers can have an effective influence on policy, especially agricultural investment[1].

It examined the current state of play of investments in African agriculture from the perspective of African farmers; it discussed key principles for investments that will strengthen family farming and sustainable food systems; and proposed actions to influence decisions.

In this context, the deliberations in the workshop were divided into 4 themes: 1) Family farming and food systems; 2) Agricultural investment strategies of the international community and the implications for family farming; 3) Farmers' organisations and processes to design and implement policies and support programmes: what participation/involvement and what outcomes?; 4) Next steps – priority action plans, calendar, actors and organisations, resources.

The methodology for the workshop used three approaches in dealing with each area of the agenda. First, each region described the situation of investments and family farming in order to provide a shared basis of knowledge and understanding, and facilitate the formulation of positions to be proposed and defended. Secondly, on the basis of these inputs, and those provided by the NGOs present, there was an analysis of the perspectives of family farming and the challenges that it faces, in order to address investment needs in a relevant manner, taking into account the programmes that are currently underway, their results and their limitations. Thirdly, contributions to an action plan were proposed. These were to provide a road map and suggest how to disseminate and build upon on the conclusions of the workshop, strengthening farmers' organisations and PAFO in its work on the sensitisation of its members, its interface with governments and development partners and its advocacy in relevant forums.

In the context of the discussions about defending productive and resilient family farming systems that currently provide food for more than 80% of the African population and could

---

[1] *The definition of 'farmers' in this meeting was meant as an term that includes the women and men, peasant and other family farmers, livestock keepers and pastoralists, fisher peoples and other fisherfolk, forest dwellers, indigenous peoples and other small-scale food providers, in both rural and urban areas. Similarly 'agriculture' was used in a broad sense to refer to multiple systems of food and non-food production, gathering and harvesting in both rural and urban areas, through farming, livestock raising, pastoralism, fisheries, aquaculture, gardening and collection of forest products.*

deliver more, the workshop summarised the analysis, in the different regions, of the state of agricultural investments in Africa and their impacts on family farming and sustainable food systems and food sovereignty, and determined collective actions.

Summary Outcomes:

The FO platforms commit to increase their knowledge and strengthen and deepen their analysis of investment dynamics and share information with their members and other networks in PAFO. They intend to find ways to increase the capacity of the networks to make the united voices of farmers' organisations heard at all levels, and to defend the interests of all Africa's family farmers, in decision making forums.

They also commit to develop and defend, in different national, regional, continental and international forums, the advocacy strategies which are urgently needed to redirect agricultural investments and defend family farming, sustainable food systems and food sovereignty. The workshop has initiated a process to determine, in different regions, the typology of family farming and its development and support needs and to share this across the continent. The processes of engagement in decision making - nationally, regionally, continentally and internationally – will be promoted especially using the approach adopted by the UN Committee on world Food Security (CFS). In this context the Chair of the Pan African Farmers' Organisation (PAFO) is encouraged to set up a working group to provide information and analysis on key issues concerning agricultural investment, other agricultural policies and related issues.

The farmers' platforms conclude that in order to defend and promote family farming, sustainable food systems and food sovereignty, it is necessary:

1. to realise a common approach in the face of harmful agricultural investments that are capturing productive resources, imposing industrial models of production, and implementing policies, strategies and research and other programmes that undermine local food systems;
2. to redirect agricultural investments towards more agroecological, biodiverse and resilient models of production supported by participatory research, development and extension systems under farmers' control;
3. to give priority to agricultural investments that support the infrastructure and input requirements of sustainable family farming;
4. to secure agricultural investments to improve the effectiveness, capacities and capabilities of farmers' organisations and networks, including their ability of farmers to self organize, for example in co-operatives that have social, economic, welfare and equity principles;
5. to ensure that there is meaningful participation by our networks and organisations, by using in particular, the approach agreed by States for civil society engagement in the Committee on World Food Security (CFS) which recognizes the autonomy of civil society organizations and welcomes them – small-scale food producers in particular – as full participants. Existing arrangements in, for example, the accelerated CAADP and other investment programmes, are not as effective.

2. Investment in Agriculture in Africa: the context: opportunities and challenges

The food crisis has opened a window of opportunity by provoking a rethinking of investment strategies to attain sustainable food security but has not yet resulted in a decisive re-orientation of approaches.

Food insecurity in Africa is a structural issue.

Food insecurity in Africa is the result of three decades of failed policies that have cut back public support to agriculture while opening African markets to unfair competition from underpriced, subsidized food products from abroad. Investment in agriculture, drastically reduced, has been oriented towards export crops targeting the global market rather than food crops for domestic consumption. It has promoted the growth of industrial systems that poison the environment and rob land and water from peasants, pastoralists and artisanal fisherfolk.

The food price crisis has provoked a range of contrasting strategy proposals

The food price crisis, with its impact on national security, has sounded a wake-up call. There is today a general recognition on the part of governments and institutions of the imperative of food security, the need to increase investment in agriculture, to strengthen domestic food production especially in food deficit countries, to address risk and resilience issues such as climate change and price volatility. But very different strategies are being proposed to meet these goals.

Most governments and institutions recognize, at least in words, the need to support small-scale producers as key actors in achieving food security. Some link food security to climate change and poverty reduction. They acknowledge the role of sustainable family farming - as compared with industrial agriculture - in creating employment, stimulating local economies and providing environmental services.[2] Others, however, place the accent on increased productivity using industrial technologies as the key factor in attaining food security. They tend to view family farming as an archaic mode of production, incapable of feeding Africa's population, that needs to be "modernized" through a transition to market-led industrial agri-food systems in which some small-scale producers could participate through contractual arrangements.[3]

Most forget that family farmers account for the bulk of Africa's food

Most governments and institutions – both in Africa and internationally – tend to ignore the evidence that African family farmers NOW are meeting up to 80% of Africa's food needs, despite the fact that they are receiving little or no policy and programme support. This blindness is compounded by a tendency to separate out investment from the issue of what agricultural models are most suited to meet food security, environmental, poverty reduction objectives. Yet an increasing body of reports, like those of the Special Rapporteur on the Right to Food and the International Assessment on Agricultural Knowledge, Science and Technology[4], document the fact that small-scale producers adopting agro-ecological approaches are capable of delivering sufficient food for the growing population as well as ensuring improved equity and a restored environment.

Rhetoric is most often not matched by action

The rhetoric about the need to invest in agriculture to combat food insecurity is not being matched by action. Some African governments, like those of Burkina Faso did take steps to support food production by family farmers in the wake of the 2008 food price crisis, with quite positive results. Nonetheless, the commitment to devote at least 10% of the national budget to agriculture adopted by African Heads of State and Government

---

[2] *See, for example, the EC policy framework to assist developing countries in addressing food security challenges. http://ec.europa.eu/development/icenter/repository/COMM_PDF_COM_2010_0127_EN.PDF*

[3] *See, for example, the "New Vision for Agriculture" of the World Economic Forum http://www3.weforum.org/docs/IP/AM11/CO/WEF_AgricultureNewVision_Roadmap_2011.pdf and the SAGCOT proposal for Tanzania www.africacorridors.com/sagcot/.*

[4] *See IAASTD documents at www.iaastd.net, and explanations and commentaries in "Agriculture at a Crossroads" - report of a conference in the UK Parliament www.ukfg.org.uk . See report on agroecology and the right to food byProf Oliver De Schutter, theUN Special Rapporteur on the Right to Food, at www.srfood.org/images/stories/pdf/officialreports/20110308_a-hrc-16-49_agroecology_en.pdf*

at the AU Summit in Maputo in 2003 has been met by less than a handful of governments. Some national and regional agriculture policies place family farming and food sovereignty at the centre of their strategies[5], yet there is a broad gap between these policies and the programmes formulated to implement them. For example, the EAC has an ARD strategy and policy that was adopted more than 5 years ago but is still relatively unimplemented, despite the persistent drought cycles in the region, with some countries in the region issuing export bans of agriculture commodities to their neighbours notwithstanding that they are implementing a full customs union and have already ratified a common market protocol that allows for free movement of goods and services.

On the side of the international community, donor ODA pledges have not been followed by disbursements. Meeting in L'Aquila in 2008 the G8 pledged $22 billion of investment in agriculture in developing countries for the 2009-2011 period, of which only $6.7 billion proved to be new, additional resources. By the time of the AFSI meeting in Paris in April 2011 disbursements amounted to only $4.2 billion. Those programmes that have been funded by ODA have most often not applied significantly different approaches to better target food security and small-scale producers.[6]

New sources of investment have appeared alongside of ODA and government expenditure

New forms of private and private/public investment have come on the scene strongly. Targeting different objectives than those of food security, poverty reduction, development, they are driven by a range of interests ranging from political (desire of rich food deficit countries to outsource food production) to commercial (for example biofuels), to financial speculation (for example hedging by investment funds). They are resulting in the commodification of African land and water resources, most visibly in the form of landgrabs. Competition for growing African urban food markets (one of few growing food markets in the world) is also on the horizon.

African governments are tending to compete to obtain these new investment flows by offering cheap and easy access to resources. In this they are aided by permissive investment regulations promoted under Bilateral Investment Treaties and the policy advice of the International Finance Corporation of the –World Bank group. Unaccountable governance and corruption is also an issue. The collusion among Foreign Direct Investment, national authorities and national capital is widespread but insufficiently documented. There is also collusion between corporate interests and development partners and philanthropic foundations that act as front runners for multilateral corporations in areas like that of introducing the products of biotechnology research and permissive bio-safety regulations.

Lots of noise about FDI and ODA but most investment is made by farmers themselves

There is increasing recognition that role of FDI and ODA in agricultural investment is marginal. What counts is in-country government investment and above all investment by family farmers themselves, which accounts for the bulk of investments in agriculture.[7] According to statistics, in 2007 out of a total of $189 billion investment in agriculture, of which $139 billion were from domestic sources (public and on-farm). Only $3 billion were attributed to FDI. It follows that what can make the most difference in terms of food security is to design an enabling policy and regulatory environment and ensure public investments in key public goods to encourage and enhance the effectiveness of family farmers' on-farm investment.

Who decides what policies and investments to promote?

As detailed in section 5 below, the family farmers' movements in Africa have built up their organizational strength and their capacity to advance and defend alternative development and investment proposals within

---

[5] *For example, the ECOWAS regional agricultural policy, ECOWAP, and the national Agricultural Framework Document of Mali.*

[6] *An example is provided by the Global Agriculture and Food Security Programme (GAFSP- www.gafspfund.org) administered by the World Bank, which up to now has tended to support activities which is are gap-fillers or scaling up of programmes already being executed by the World Bank and Regional Development Banks. The civil society members of the GAFSP Steering Committee are advocating for a revision of the call criteria of the GAFSP to privilege objectives of food security and support to family farmers.*

[7] *This will be a major message of the 2012 issue of FAO's The State of Food and Agriculture (SOFA), dedicated to investment in agriculture.*

the framework of food sovereignty. They are now capable of representing the interests of the primary agricultural investors in reflections and negotiations regarding agricultural investment, but they are not sufficiently involved in decision-making at all levels. Stakeholder participation is intended to be a key component of the CAADP process, but the race towards investments is accelerating the CAADP compact and Country Investment Plan process to such a degree that stakeholder participation and impact on policy and programme design and implementation becomes increasingly difficult.

At regional, continental and global levels there is a multiplication of proposals for guidelines, codes of conduct, and principles relevant to agricultural investment at all levels. Only a few of these – notably the FAO Voluntary Guidelines on Governance of Land and Natural Resource Tenure – involve the actors most concerned in the process of formulation in a meaningful way. Others, like the RAI Principles formulated by the World Bank, FAO, IFAD and UNCTAD, have seen no involvement by civil society actors (or governments) and risk legitimizing unaccountable decisions on private and private/public investment to the detriment of family farmers and sustainable food systems. The reformed Committee on World Food Security (CFS), in which family farmers' organizations are full and active participants, provides a potential opportunity to bring food security concerns to bear on strategies for investment in agriculture.

3. Family farming in Africa : concepts, realities and potential to strengthen sustainable food systems

Preliminary considerations

In order to discuss family farming meaningfully it is necessary to define the **objectives** of agriculture in Africa. This has not yet been done in the many African countries that have not adopted a national agricultural policy. When such an exercise of strategic orientation is undertaken a number of other key questions emerge which must also be addressed, among others:

- What kind(s) of market(s) should be created or promoted, with which actors?
- What kinds of accompanying measures are necessary to add value to the products?
- What other social, cultural, economic and environmental services, apart from production alone, do African societies want agriculture to provide?

Family farming must be analysed in a holistic and multifunctional fashion. When this kind of broader framework is applied the advantages of sustainable family farming as compared with industrial agriculture become overwhelmingly evident, as documented in a growing body of studies.

What do we mean by family farming and family farms?

It can be useful to start off by demolishing some misleading myths. Family farming is **not** an archaic model of agriculture, imprisoned in impossibly tiny farm sizes and frozen into a declining destiny of subsistence production. On the contrary it is a diversified and constantly evolving model which is perfectly capable of increasing its already substantial contribution to the food security and the economic, social and environmental well-being of African countries and regions.

Family farming is a way of life as well as a mode of production. It is opposed to the model of industrial agriculture by its objectives in the first instance. While industrial agriculture aims only at generating profits from financial capital, the primary objective of family farming is the reproduction of the family unit through food production for household consumption and, successively, the generation of revenues to meet the other needs of its members.

By definition, a **family farm** is a human unit/entity of production in which the farmers (and their associates) apply a system of agricultural production.

Agricultural units can be classified into two categories which are associated with two modes of production that have very different bases:
- family farms ;
- industrial agricultural enterprises (agribusiness and agro-industry).

58

The **family farm** could be defined as follows:

An <u>association</u> **composed of two or more members united by family or customary ties, which exploits production factors in common - in rural or urban areas - in order to generate resources (for social reproduction as well as financial, material, moral resources…). The family farm operates under the direction of one of its members, male or female. Its priority is to produce food for the members of the unit and, successively, to create wealth in order to contribute to their well-being.**

The head of the unit is responsible for managing the farm's activities and ensuring the best possible exploitation of the factors of production while respecting the environment. He or she exercises this function as his/her principle occupation. The members of the unit – men, women, and young people - have the responsibility of working to achieve the economic and social viability of the farm.

In other words:
A family farm is a group of people with family ties who produce, while protecting the environment, in order to feed themselves in the first instance and to provide the surplus to the local market or elsewhere in order to earn income to improve their living conditions. It is directed by a man or woman member of the farm.

Basic principles

There is a variety of typologies of family farming both among African regions and within each region. Mapping these typologies and the kinds of policy and programme/investment support they require is a priority engagement of the African regional farmers' platforms. However, family farming throughout Africa responds to a set of basic principles which are interrelated and cannot be dissociated:

- The model of agriculture promoted by family farms aims at feeding its members as a first priority and then at generating income.
- It is a model which – unlike industrial agriculture – allows for working in harmony with the environment by respecting the principles of sustainability based on agro-ecological modes of production.;
- It creates sustainable employment both for the members of the unit and for others outside of the farm, like local artisans and small-scale traders.
- It systematically promotes the diversification of production. By placing priority on minimizing risks rather than maximizing profits it combats the industrial monoculture systems which destroy the environment;
- It contributes to organizing local food markets according to an approach by levels: from the household on up to the village, the commune or district, the region, and so on. It contributes to social economy and solidarity by promoting a better redistribution of the resources generated ;
- It promotes participatory research within the production space and carries out on-going professional training structured around the farm activities and mode of life;
- The means of production are under the control of the members of the farm;
- It is oriented towards the attainment of food sovereignty and the respect of human dignity.

Family farming and Africa's food needs

Family farms produce up to 80% of the food consumed in African countries, much of which does not enter the formal market. They provide employment for 70% of the population, both directly and by stimulating local economies, and constitute the only potential solution for absorbing the growing population of unemployed young people. They use a large proportion of cultivated, fallow and grazed land[8] and are responsible for the sustainable management of the bulk of Africa's natural resources. They constitute a response to the risks of food price volatility. Research conducted in Senegal demonstrates that family farms produce two-thirds of all of food consumed in Senegal today and practically all of the dry cereals that constitute the staple food of more than 60% of the population.[9] If they benefited from the necessary political, economic and social accompanying measures they would be able to feed Africa's growing population in a sustainable fashion and contribute to a more vibrant and equitable economy.

---

[8] *See Joan Baxter, 7 April 2011 "The War On Africa's Family Farmers" http://allafrica.com/stories/201104080804.html*
[9] *"Les exploitations familiales ont la capacité de nourrir le Sénégal" -
www.cncr.org/IMG/pdf/forum_paysan_message_1_texte_1_.pdf*

4. <u>Constraints and Proposals</u>

As described in the previous section, African family farmers and their sustainable food systems are able to feed Africa and more, given adequate protection and support, and this could be enhanced by a redirection of agricultural investments. The key question is therefore: How to ensure that agricultural investments are directed towards the model of production that is embodied in family farming?

A number of other questions were raised in the workshop, which highlight the key challenges that confront family farming, including:

- How can access by family farmers to land and other productive resources be secured without promoting the privatisation of the country's land?
- How can the visibility of family farming be enhanced and consumer choices be directed towards local products in the face of the loss of traditional food habits as a result of food aid, dumped food imports etc?
- How can priority be given to an approach that focuses on overall income for family farms rather than one based on prices, which does not take into account the expenses that family famers incur that allow the farm family to feed itself as well as generate sufficient income for basic social services such as education, health, housing and water?
- How can local, national and regional markets be organised in such a way as to better integrate family farming into a economic system based on social solidarity, which creates employment and redistributes wealth?
- How can research be developed towards agroecological methods and techniques, in a participatory way, to give priority to the production, processing and provision of local foods produced sustainably by family farms? How can the results of this research be better shared at the level of family farmers to facilitate the adoption of innovative production techniques? How can information provision support family farming and sustainable food systems?
- How can technical assistance and extension be organised so that it supports family farming – both production and local processing which adds value?
- How can coherent agricultural policies be developed in the framework of food sovereignty?
- How can farmers' organisations, platforms and networks defend themselves from the imposed creation of parallel structures, by states, NGOs and international programmes, that will undermine a coherent voice in support of family farming and sustainable food systems by our established networks?

Following detailed discussions, participants identified four sets of constraints which have been summarised below; and made a non-exhaustive set of proposals of how to deal withy these. In addition there was a fifth constraint – that of 'participation' – and it is dealt with separately in the subsequent section.

Constraint:
- In the face of widespread land and water 'grabs', the privatisation of natural resources and farmers' seeds and other resources as well as various threats to natural resources such as the degradation of soils and the reduction in grazing lands, climate change impacts, family farmers must be able to secure access to and control over the means of production – land, water, seeds and agricultural biodiversity, energy – especially for women and youth, that are necessary to strengthen family farming.

Proposal
To realise this, the coherent resistance across the regions is needed to confront the capture, commodification and privatisation of resources and that policies, in the framework of food sovereignty, should be developed at national and regional levels to protect the resources for, and increase the resilience of, agroecological production[10], necessary for family farming now and in the future.

---

[10] *The necessary move towards agroecological production is one that would integrate cropping, livestock raising and fisheries in the production system, where possible*

Constraint:

- The shortage of long-term credit, funding and insurance to support, especially women, family farmers, pastoralism and artisanal fishing is a major constraint. What is currently available does not address the priority needs of family farmers, which funders do not recognise and understand.

Proposal

Dedicated funds at affordable costs should be made available for the long-term support of family farming and the supply of inputs needed to realise their sustainable food systems e.g. locally adapted and biodiverse seeds, diverse breeding stock, biopesticides, organic manures, appropriate equipment for tillage, irrigation and transport, and sustainable, especially bio-, energy sources.

Constraint:

- The availability of, and access to, appropriate markets for surplus products, and those grown or raised or harvested sustainably for national and regional markets, is very limited. The transport infrastructure does not serve family farms in many areas. Regional integration of policies and practices for the free movement of people and goods is problematic. Locally produced foods struggle to compete with imported subsidised products: local production is unprotected. Inadequate storage facilities on-farm, locally and nationally limit ability to realise price stabilisation. Supply management policies are weak or non-existent.

Proposal

Investments should be directed to improving and facilitating access to local, national and regional markets, including those which are transboundary, and trade and other policies to stabilise prices and protect family farming should be introduced. Improvements in the organisation of family farmers' and smallholder organisations – especially their ability to self organize- should be encouraged. The appropriate types of organisation include a co-operative models that have social, economic, welfare and equity principles. They are a vehicle for sustainable rural development approaches and can be entities that will improve access to credit, agriculture advisory services, warehousing, postharvest, bulking and marketing etc. EAFF has already prepared and presented a regional policy framework on co-operatives to EAC and currently to COMESA for consideration and adoption by their respective council of Ministers.

Constraint:

- The limited availability of appropriate capacity building at different levels and the necessary institutional infrastructure was highlighted as a major constraint. Training centres are needed to develop skills necessary to develop family farming and local markets and the capacity for effective lobbying. This constraint contributes to the weak involvement of farmers' platforms and networks in developing, following and monitoring policies and strategies that should be redirected towards realising a sustainable food system provided by family farming and in the implementation of farming and rural development projects in support of this. Capacity is limited for developing farmers' own proposals for realising this shift in policy and practice.

Proposal

To realise improved capacity for the diversification of biodiverse, ecological and resilient family farming, requires improved formal (institution based) and informal (on-farm) training, farmer to farmer extension systems, improved information systems as well as the development of improved policy and lobbying capacities at national and regional levels.

5. Participation: improving African farmer organizations' participation in, and impact on, the design and implementation of agricultural policies and investment programmes.

Family farmers throughout Africa have reacted to the onslaught of structural adjustment and neo-liberal policies by developing a variety of strategies to defend their local food systems and by building up their organizations from the national to the regional and continental levels. Today, family farmers' networks exist and interact with governments and intergovernmental institutions at national level and regionally; ROPPA in West Africa, PROPAC in Central Africa, EAFF in East Africa, SACAU in Southern Africa. In October 2010 these four platforms, along with UMAGRI in the Magreb, came together in Malawi to constitute the Pan-African Farmers' Organization (PAFO), which has been recognised by the African Union.

Participatory formulation of agricultural policies and investment programmes – and the CAADP process - have been a strong focus of the farmer platforms' fight to achieve meaningful involvement in decision-making. Already in 2004 the four SSA farmers' platforms submitted to NEPAD their concerted vision of agriculture in the context of CAADP. Since then they have continued to deepen their platforms of proposals based on sustainable family farming and increased control over their food systems in a framework of food sovereignty.[11] They have defended these platforms in forums from the national to the global level, on issues ranging from agricultural policies to trade (e.g. EPAs and WTO), access to natural resources, biodiversity, research, the formulation and implementation of agricultural sector programmes, and others.

These efforts have met with a certain degree of success. Farmers' platforms have been enabled in some countries and regions to organize consultative processes in order to feed farmers' views into the formulation of agricultural policies and land tenure and pastoral codes.[12] In some cases national farmer platforms have been able to obtain the reformulation of Country Investment Programmes in whose formulation they were not involved and which did not respond to objectives of food security and poverty reduction.[13] In these cases key factors have been the ability to speak with one voice and to build strong alliances with other actors. Calling government officials and elected representatives to account has also been effective.

But much more needs to be done. Farmers' platforms need to be able to go beyond generic defence of family farming to develop their own proposals for alternative policies and programmes that strengthen their sustainable food systems rather than co-opting them into agro-industrial systems. They need to defend their autonomy against official efforts to create parallel platforms and to divide the movement. At the same time, to ensure integrity, the legitimate organisations and networks of family farmers must achieve accountability and transparency in leadership at all levels.

There is a need for opening up agriculture policy processes to more diverse views and forms of knowledge derived from farmers and their organisations and for these processes to embrace participatory decision-making approaches in the policy-making and agenda setting as well. Much has been written about the kind of inclusive deliberative processes that can ensure meaningful and decisive participation[14]. A significant achievement by civil society, including especially farmers' movements, in the process of reform of the UN/FAO Committee on world Food Security (CFS), has been the recognition of civil society's right to autonomously develop an inclusive and self-organised process for interacting with the member governments and the CFS as a whole– the Civil Society Mechanism (CSM).[15] In the CFS, all participants – including civil society - engage in the debate on an equal footing but it is member governments that are responsible and accountable for making decisions.

There is a need to realise this standard of meaningful engagement in all policy making forums including those focused on agricultural investment decisions in and for Africa. Recognizing that the same issues are raised at different levels – from local to global – and in a variety of different forums, it is necessary to develop multi-level strategies of engagement that can enable farmers' platforms and their allies to defend coherent common platforms of claims and proposals wherever there is an opportunity to have an impact.

---

[11] *See the Declaration and Synthesis Report of the Nyéléni 2007 Forum for Food Sovereignty (www.nyeleni.org). See also www.roppa.info, http://eaffu.org; www.sacau.info*

[12] *For example in Senegal, Mali, ECOWAS.*

[13] *For example, Burundi and Benin.*

[14] *See, for example, publications by McKeon and Pimbert*

[15] *See website of CSOs in the CFS/CSM process: http://.cso4cfs.org.*

To achieve this, the recommendations concerning participation are:

- Improve capacity building for policy and investment programme processes (including formulation, interpretation, analysis, tracking and reporting) at all levels, both within and outside of the farmers' networks.
- Advocate the establishment at all levels of inclusive institutional frameworks in which the roles and responsibilities of all actors are clearly defined.
- At country and regional levels, the farmers organisations will strive to improve their ability to make their own proposals on agriculture investments and table them during national or regional debates/ discussions on investments in a coherent manner that will be mutually supportive across the movement.
- While respecting diversity of views in different platforms and countries, a common platform through PAFO will help ensure coherence in engagement in processes and proposals made at all levels.
- In the context of PAFO, develop a system of information sharing among regional platforms and of drawing on the human resources available in the platforms and in partner organizations.
- Strengthen economic resources of farmers' platforms to ensure autonomous, self-organising capacities at national/regional/continental levels.
- Strengthening alliances with CSOs, other FOs and like minded organizations in Africa and other regions[16]
- Increasing knowledge at all levels including individual famers' organisations to national platforms and the regional and continental networks about the CFS/CSM process and ensuring continuity in engagement and follow-up.

---

[16] *Alliances include: EuropAfrica; More and Better network; IPC for food sovereignty; CFS/CSM*

6. Action Plan

In the context of the discussions about defending our productive and resilient family farming system that currently provides food for more than 80% of the African population and could deliver more, we commit to sharing our analysis of the state of agricultural investments in Africa and their impacts on our family farming and sustainable food systems and food sovereignty with our members and other networks in PAFO. We highlight the following points:

1. We will work with our networks and organisations across all regions to realise a common approach to defending family farming and sustainable food systems in the face of harmful agricultural investments that are capturing productive resources, which should be available to family farmers, commodifying and privatising these, imposing industrial models of production tied to mainly industrial input and market channels, and the promulgation of policies, strategies and research and other programmes that undermine our food systems.

2. We propose that agricultural investments are redirected towards developing and realising more agroecological, biodiverse and resilient models of production, in particular for local consumption, which should be proposed by farmers' organisations, supported by appropriate participatory research, development and extension systems under their control.

3. We want to ensure that priority is given to agricultural investments that support infrastructure requirements for family farming and sustainable food systems, to provide the inputs needed, and to ensure that markets for local (and often healthier) products are prioritised and protected.

4. We need resources from agricultural investments to improve the effectiveness, capacities and capabilities of our organisations and networks at all levels to be able to develop, promote and defend family farming, our sustainable food systems and food sovereignty, including their ability of our farmers to self organize, for example in co-operatives that have social, economic, welfare and equity principles.

5. We urge that all decision making forums about agricultural investments and related policies, at all levels, ensure that there is meaningful participation by our networks and organisations, by using, in particular, the approach agreed by States for civil society engagement in the Committee on World Food Security (CFS). Existing arrangements in, for example, the accelerated CAADP and other investment programmes, are not effective in ensuring the defence of family farming and our sustainable food systems.

Specific actions:

*   Encourage the Chair of PAFO to set up a working group to provide information and analysis on key issues concerning agricultural investment, other agricultural policies and related issues.

*   Share the outputs of this workshop with regional networks and member organisations and deepen the debate and understanding of challenges and the core concepts presented e.g. the typology of family farming and its development and defence; and the processes of engagement nationally, regionally, continentally and internationally, including the approach used in the CFS.

*   Develop processes, including a continental workshop, to strategise, develop and take further the advocacy strategies, in different national, regional and international forums, which are urgently needed to redirect agricultural investments and defend family farming, our sustainable food systems and food sovereignty.

Steps to translate into action the vision of the African farmers' organizations regarding family farming and agricultural investment

Action to be undertaken	By whom and at what level	Targets	By when
Finalise the synthesis report and send to the regional platforms and for translation	Workshop Steering Committee		10 May 2011
Feedback from the regional platforms and validation of the synthesis report	EAFF PROPAC ROPPA		16 May 2011
Reflection of the typology of family farms and their support needs	EAFF PROPAC ROPPA SACAU UMAGRI	Farmers' organisations Public institutions Private sector Research institutes Development partners	2011
Continental workshop to harmonize the concept of family farming leading to drafting of a position paper/advocacy document	PAFO	Regional platforms (EAFF, PROPAC, ROPPA, SACAU, UMAGRI)	2011
Advocacy directed to African and international institutions	EAFF PROPAC ROPPA SACAU UMAGRI PAFO with allies.	AU and specialized institutions NEPAD Regional Economic Organizations and specialized institutions, including the African Development Bank FAO IFAD World Bank CFS EU G20	On-going (see partial list of up-coming meetings, events, forums and processes in Annex 3)

Annex 3

a CPRE campaign briefing

Mapping Local Food Webs:
methodology and survey

Mapping the complex links between local producers, services and communities provides a powerful tool that can help safeguard local economies.

CPRE

Your countryside
your voice

Introduction

By processing and retailing goods locally significant benefits can be secured for the economies of rural areas, revitalising rural communities, increasing employment and supporting investment in a beautiful and environmentally diverse landscape.[1]

Mapping local food webs is a vital part of CPRE's local food campaign, which aims to increase support for the local food sector in order that its wider benefits can be realised. Related publications you may find useful to refer to are CPRE's local food campaign briefing, *Local Action for Local Foods*[2]; CPRE's *Food Webs* report[3]; and *Sustainable Local Foods* campaign briefing[4].

The food webs survey is designed to be used locally to demonstrate the important web of links that make up local food economies. This can highlight the interdependent relationship between networks of local producers, processors, wholesalers, shops and services and the way they contribute to the local food economy and support the local community.

The range of opportunities in which this survey methodology can be useful are endless. This includes everything from demonstrating the impact of a proposed supermarket development in order to oppose the application, to making a case for the installation of new facilities such as processing or cutting plants – the lack of which are holding back what could be a thriving local food economy.

Food webs

A food webs survey in rural Suffolk, carried out by Caroline Cranbrook in response to an application by a major supermarket, revealed detailed information about the local food economy. This provided sound evidence demonstrating the potential threat to the local food economy and community with the result that the supermarket withdrew its application. This was documented in the CPRE report, *Food Webs*[5], and other similar surveys have been carried out elsewhere by CPRE local groups.

---

1 CPRE, *Sustainable Local Foods*, September 2001
2 CPRE, *Local Action for Local Foods*, May 2002
3 CPRE, *Food Webs*, reprinted March 2002
4 CPRE, *Sustainable Local Foods*, September 2001
5 CPRE, *Food Webs*, reprinted March 2002

CPRE's Local Foods Campaign

The local food sector is expanding rapidly and the income from sustainable local food, from farmers' markets to organic box schemes, is becoming increasingly significant for local economies. The wider benefits of local foods are well recognised; they:

- provide an additional source of income for farmers;

- give consumers greater knowledge about, access to, and choice of food;

- benefit the environment and offer ways of valuing the local landscape;

- bring social and economic advantages to rural and urban communities; and

- strengthen local economies and local employment opportunities.

Consumers are becoming increasingly discerning in their food choices and are demanding safe, environmentally and welfare friendly food. Sustainable local food initiatives are also delivering greater accessibility to healthy, affordable food to some of the poorest areas and can directly tackling health inequalities[6].

There is considerable scope for local volunteers, working with local authorities and a variety of different stakeholders, to encourage growth of local food economies. This is essential in order to encourage change from the grass roots and overcome some of the barriers that may be hindering the development of the local food sector. Mapping local food webs can be a useful tool to help deliver change locally and increase support for a strong local food economy.

---

6   CPRE, *Sustainable Local Foods*, September 2001

Food Webs Mapping

Why use the food webs survey?

Mapping local food webs is a powerful tool. It can provide important evidence demonstrating the intricate web of local food networks, their economic impact and subsequent money flows. It highlights where local food initiatives encourage the use of local producers, processors, suppliers and retailers and how this can help retain the economic benefit of businesses within the immediate area, as well as reducing the distance travelled by goods. This in turn generates more economic activity and jobs and demand for other local services.

When to use the food webs survey

The growth of strong local food economies can be effectively supported at a local and regional level and there are a range of instances in which mapping local food webs could prove a useful and effective campaigning tool to achieve this. See CPRE's campaign briefing, *Local Action for Local Foods*[7] for further ideas. For example, you may want to:

- **encourage greater support for existing local food initiatives**: a local authority may want to consider funding a local food development post to identify and solve the logistical problems local food producers are facing. The food webs survey produces evidence of the tangible benefits of strong local food economies and the barriers that need to be overcome to allow growth in the sector;

- **promote new initiatives or projects**: a Local Authority or local business may consider supporting the introduction of a farmers' market. A food webs survey of another farmers' market may provide the evidence they need to make a case for support;

- **enforce stronger controls against potentially damaging out of town developments**: the food webs survey was pioneered in Suffolk to successfully oppose a damaging supermarket development by highlighting the potential job losses and threats to the local economy, community and the environment by the proposed development;

- **strengthen local business networks between consumers, producers, suppliers and retailers**: use the food webs survey to demonstrate the significance of these inter-connections which often underpin the viability of local economies and communities;

- **ensure policy makers are aware of the effects changes in service delivery can have, particularly on rural areas**: the food webs survey can

---

7   CPRE, *Local Action for Local Foods*, May 2002

illustrate not only the reach and complexity of the local food economy but its vulnerability to particular changes;

- **raise public awareness of the opportunities brought by local food initiatives and the problems facing them**: the success of the local food sector relies on an exchange of information and understanding between the producer and the consumer, leading to a more sustainable food economy. The food webs survey can help trace the movement of food and 'tell the story' of a local food, and this guide gives some suggestions as to how to get the message across to the general public.

How to use the food webs survey

What do I need to do to carry out a food webs survey?

The food webs survey is a fairly simple but effective tool, and you will need to:

- identify a survey area and, if not yourself, someone to carry out the survey;

- carry out the survey, which involves a number of interviews with, for example, local shops, businesses, processors or producers;

- collate the survey findings and preparing a short report of the survey;

- use the survey to influence local or regional decision-making.

How much time do I need?

The survey need not take up too much time or effort - this largely depends on the size of the area you want to cover and what detail you need to go into. Caroline Cranbrook estimates that it took her a few afternoons over a period of 2 weeks to survey 81 businesses in seven market towns. This was followed by a couple of mornings spent pulling the results together.

Where should surveys be conducted?

A survey can be carried out anywhere, bearing in mind larger settlements may need more time as the business networks may be more complex. You could also survey a group of smaller settlements, or, if there is a proposal for a new supermarket development it may be sensible to concentrate on the area in the supermarket's impact study.

Getting started

When you have decided on your survey area, identify the shops and businesses within it. You do not have to survey all of these but the more you can do the more complete your picture of the situation will be. Target shops selling food and then newsagents, hardware shops, pharmacies, garages etc (if you have the time).

Choose a quiet time of day to talk to the manager or owner of the shop so that you are not distracting them from serving customers and they have the time to chat with you and answer your questions fully. Ideally you could combine the survey with your own shopping so that you can talk to the manager/owner of the shop when paying, or make an appointment to come back another time.

Make sure to explain who you are, why you are doing the survey and what you will do with the results. Reassure them that they will not be quoted or sourced without their permission.

There is quite a lot of the form that can be filled in without bothering the shop manager, for instance you could write down the range of products stocked but do make sure you have explained what you are doing first.

The survey form

The survey form has been designed for use in a general store, some of the questions may not be relevant to the shops or businesses you are surveying so do adapt the form where you think it is appropriate.

Most of the questions on the form are self-explanatory but you may want to think about the following questions:

- **post office**: is there a post office in the shop?

- **number of employees**: find out as much as possible about the employees, are they local people, how do they get to work, are they working mothers or retired people, are their hours flexible, how many hours do they work etc?

- **other people employed occasionally**: does the shop use local tradesmen, cleaners etc?

- **services provided by the shop**: does the shop sell lottery tickets, make up orders, run a delivery service, have a public notice board, collect laundry etc? Does it charge for these services? Maybe you could ask very subtly if they provide credit.

- **local services used by the shop**: find out if the shop banks locally, uses a local solicitor, local newspaper for advertising etc.

- **estimate of distance regular customers travel to use shop**: obviously there will not be hard figures available but the manger may have an impression of whether it is just villagers that use the shop or whether people travel from neighbouring villages. Are there any regular customers who do not own a car?

- **range of products stocked and sources of supply**: some products such as eggs, meat and dairy products will probably have details of their origins on their packaging. With other products it may be easiest to go around the shop with the owner and source all the major items, fruit and vegetables, baked goods. You may wish to consider the following:

- find out what, if any, local wholesalers and cash and carries the shop uses. Some wholesalers have ranges of local goods so check this and don't assume that products bought from a wholesaler aren't local.

- find out if they have their supplies delivered or do they collect them themselves?

- most importantly, if they stock local produce, try to get the name of the producer (some retailers and suppliers may be sensitive to reveal certain information so don't pursue this too far if the shop owner seems reluctant).

- maybe the shop does its own baking, smoking, sausage-making etc.

- remember to find out about other local products used e.g. packaging material; and

- check if the shop sells other things that aren't on display e.g. firewood, videos, charcoal, seasonal items such as Christmas trees etc.

- **notes**: include any impressions you have of the shop, whether it seems busy, does the staff know the customers, are customers walking, cycling, driving to the shop etc. If you have time you could also consider following-up supply chains and talking to producers and wholesalers.

Compiling and Analysing Survey Findings

Particularly useful data to put together would be:

- numbers of people employed – full and part time;

- range of services available;

- number of inter-related local businesses i.e. shops, producers, wholesalers, banks etc;

- sphere of influence of all the shops;

  - distance to other businesses;

  - distance travelled by customers;

  - distance travelled by produce;

- percentage of stock that comes from local producers;

- if a supermarket is proposed in the area is it likely to result in loss of jobs; and

- matrixes of linkages e.g. where shops are stocking locally produced goods, draw a matrix which shows how many local shops are dependent on how many local producers. This will be useful in demonstrating how, if for instance shop 1 closed, it would affect three different producers.

This information can be presented in many ways. You may wish to compile just a few simple figures for a press release or you might put together a report with recommendations which could be circulated to local decision-makers and organisations concerned with local services or economic development or used to help encourage local service providers improve the services they offer. The various possibilities of getting your message across are outlined below.

Getting Your Message Across

Having completed the survey you need to tell everyone about your findings to help ensure that for instance local shops and services are safeguarded and the local food economy is strengthened in ways that do not damage the countryside. There are a number of important audiences to consider. These include the media, decision-makers and the wider public.

The media: issuing a local press release

Issuing a press release announcing the findings of the survey (e.g. the number of jobs and businesses supported by the local economic network) or drawing attention to the problems facing rural services in the area will help to bring the issue to the attention of local decision-makers and raise CPRE's profile locally.

Local decision-makers: letter writing

Having spent so much time and effort on the survey it is important to make sure that local decision-makers know your views about local services and rural development. As such, you may want to write to:

- the Regional Development Agency;

- the Government Office for the Region: contact the rural division;

- local authority officers: those responsible for planning, retailing and economic development at the County Council and District Council;

- local councillors;

- the local MP;

- local rural development organisations such as the Chamber of Commerce or the local trade association; and

- other local community organisations such as the Parish Council or the Rural Community Council.

The letter should be sent not later than the embargo date of your press release. As well as highlighting the findings of your survey you should suggest a number of things which need to happen next. This could include: greater financial support or advice for local rural businesses; help in marketing local products; or stronger controls on out-of-town development.

The general public: leaflet drop

Raising general awareness about these issues is essential to the success of this campaign. The local press release will help raise local awareness of the issue and also CPRE's profile but this could be supplemented by other activities which you may want to consider. For example, if you are using the survey to campaign against a potentially damaging proposal yo could prepare a simple leaflet outlining your campaign to help drum-up extra support. This could explain the proposal, outline the impact on th local area and demonstrate why more local support is needed.

You could also highlight the decline in rural services overall (perhaps by collating some local statistics – the Countryside Agency may have local figures) and outline how CPRE can help to make a difference.

Finally, please send a copy of your results to CPRE national office.

Further Information

CPRE reports available from CPRE Publications: publications@cpre.org.uk

Local foods

CPRE, *Local Action for Local Foods*, May 2002, £3.50

CPRE, *Sustainable Local Foods*, September 2001, £3.50

CPRE, *Food Webs*, (reprinted) March 2002, available free on receipt of an A4 sae

CPRE, *Local Food in Britain: A research review for CPRE*, (MacGillivray) November 2001, available free on receipt of an A4 sae

Rural services

CPRE, *Rural Services: a framework for action*, September 1999, available free on receipt of an A4 sae

CPRE, *Rural Services Charter*, November 1998, available free on receipt of an A4 sae

Other useful references

The retail section of your Local Development Plan may contain some useful background material.

The Countryside Agency's rural services survey is available at www.countryside.gov.uk/ruralservices

Nichol, L, *How can planning help the local food economy? A guide for planners*, Oxford Brookes University, November 2001

Sustain: the alliance for better food and farming, *A Battle in store: a discussion of the social impact of the major UK supermarkets*, 2000 www.sustainweb.org

Sustain/Elm Farm Research Centre, *Eating Oil: food in a changing climate*, 2001

CPRE
Food Webs Survey

Name of surveyor:	CPRE branch/district group:	Date:

Town/village:

Name/type of business:

Address of business:

Tel:

Owner/manager:

Post office:

Major wholesaler *(eg Londis, Happy Shopper etc.)*

Opening hours – Monday – Friday	Opening hours – Saturday	Opening hours – Sunday
Number of employees – full time:	Number of employees – part time: *(include hours worked)*	Number of employees – delivering:

Other people employed occasionally *(eg carpenter)*:

How long has the shop been trading?	How long has the owner/manager run the shop?

Services offered by shop:

Local services used by shop:

Estimate of number of customers weekly:	Estimate of distance regular customers travel to use shop:

CPRE

Your countryside your voice

Range of products stocked	
Locally supplied	**Other suppliers**
Fruit, vegetables and herbs:	
Meat, fish and game:	
Cooked meats:	
Dairy *(e.g. eggs, ice-cream)*:	

Locally supplied	Other suppliers
Bread, flour and baked goods *(e.g. quiches, sausage rolls)*	
Jams, preserves, honey and sauces:	
Sandwiches:	
Tinned and packaged goods:	
Drinks *(alcoholic and soft):*	
Flowers and plants:	
Cleaning products:	
Other *(e.g. firewood, birthday cards, stationery):*	

Notes:

For more information about CPRE's Local Foods Campaign contact:

CPRE Rural Policy Team
Warwick House, 25 Buckingham Palace Road
London SW1W OPP
Tel: 020 7976 6433 Fax: 020 7976 6373
Email: info@cpre.org.uk Website: www.cpre.org.uk

CPRE is a company limited by guarantee, registered in England, number 4302973. Registered charity number: 1089685
April 2002

References

Acho-Chi, C. (2002) 'The mobile street food service practice in the urban economy of Kumba', *Cameroon Singapore Journal of Tropical Geography*, 23 (2): 131–48 <http://onlinelibrary.wiley.com/doi/10.1111/1467-9493.00122>.

Aubry, S., Seufert, P. and Monsalve Suárez, S. (2012) *(Bio)Fueling Injustice? Europe's Responsibility to Counter Climate Change Without Provoking Land Grabbing and Compounding Food Insecurity in Africa*, The EuropAfrica 2011 Monitoring Report on EU Policy Coherence for Food Security, Rome: EuropAfrica <www.europafrica. info/en/publications/biofueling-injustice> [accessed 9 August 2013].

Ayieko, M.W., Tschirley, D.L. and Mathenge, M.W. (2005) 'Fresh fruit and vegetable consumption patterns and supply chain systems in urban Kenya: implications for policy and investment priorities', Working Paper 16, Kenya: Tegemeo Institute of Agricultural Policy and Development.

Blench, R. (2001) *'You Can't Go Home Again': Pastoralism in the New Millennium*, London: Overseas Development Institute <www.odi.org.uk/sites/odi.org.uk/files/ odi-assets/publications-opinion-files/6329.pdf> [accessed 15 November 2013].

Bopda, A., Brummett, R., Dury, S., Elong, P., Foto-Menbohan, S., Gockowski, J., Kana, C., Kengue, J., Ngonthe, R., Nolte, C., Soua, N., Tanawa, E., Tchouendjeu, Z. and Temple, L. (2010) 'Urban farming systems in Yaoundé: building a mosaic' in Prain, G., Karanja, N. and Lee-Smith, D. (eds), *African Urban Harvest: Agriculture in the Cities of Cameroon, Kenya and Uganda*, New York: Springer.

Calza Bini, E. and Boccaleoni, S. (eds) (2010) Food Sovereignty: A Common Challenge in Africa and in Europe – Agricultural Policies and Regional Integration for Family Farming, Rome: EuropAfrica Campaign <www.csa-be.org/IMG/pdf_ pubbeuropafrica_eng_low.pdf> [accessed 15 November 2013].

Campaign to Protect Rural England (CPRE) (1998) 'Food webs: a report on local food networks in East Suffolk which demonstrates the importance of local shops and services to rural communities', CPRE: London <www.cpre.org.uk/resources/ farming-and-food/local-foods/item/1915-food-webs> [accessed 9 August 2013].

CPRE (2011a) 'From field to fork: Sheffield. Mapping the local food web', CPRE: London <www.cpre.org.uk/resources/farming-and-food/local-foods/item/2043- from-field-to-fork-sheffield> [accessed 4 December 2013].

CPRE (2011b) 'From field to fork: mapping the local food web', CPRE: London <www. cpre.org.uk/what-we-do/farming-and-food/local-foods/update/item/2896-local- food-is-recipe-for-economic-success> [accessed 9 August 2013].

CPRE (2012) 'Local foods' [online] <www.cpre.org.uk/resources/farming-and-food/ local-foods> [accessed 4 December 2013].

De Schutter, O. (2009) 'The right to food and the political economy of hunger', 26th McDougall Memorial Lecture, Rome, 18 November <ftp://ftp.fao.org/ docrep/fao/meeting/018/k6518e.pdf> [accessed 9 August 2013].

De Schutter, O. (2011) 'Agroecology and the right to food', presented at the 16th Session of the United Nations Human Rights Council, 8 March [A/HRC/16/49] <www.srfood.org/en/report-agroecology-and-the-right-to-food> [accessed 15 November 2013].

ETC Group (2009) 'Who will feed us? Questions for the food and climate crises', Communiqué Issue 102 <www.etcgroup.org/sites/www.etcgroup.org/files/ETC_Who_Will_Feed_Us.pdf> [accessed 9 August 2013].

Ewole, G. (2010) *Models of Production in Central Africa: Case of Cameroon,* [Place]: PROPAC.

Facilitating Alternative Agro-food Networks (FAAN) (2010) 'Local food systems in Europe: case studies from five countries and what they imply for policy and practice', FAAN <www.faanweb.eu/sites/faanweb.eu/files/FAAN_Booklet_PRINT.pdf> [accessed 9 August 2013].

FAO (2010) 'Enhancing the contribution of non-wood forest products to poverty alleviation and food security in central African countries', Information Note No. 2 <www.fao.org/docrep/012/al193e/al193e00.pdf> [accessed 11 October 2013].

Fonjong, L. and Endeley, J. (2004) 'The potentials of female micro entrepreneurial activities within the informal sector in poverty reduction in Cameroon: opportunities, constraints, and the way forward', presented at the workshop on strategy for West Africa on poverty reduction, gender, and enterprise development, Accra, Ghana, 3–6 August <http://bit.ly/rtSLpe> [accessed 12 September 2011].

Gitu, K.W. (2006) *Agricultural Development and Food Security in Sub-Saharan Africa (SSA): Building a Case for more Support: The Case of Kenya*, Working Paper No. 3, Policy Assistance Unit, FAO Subregional Office for East and Southern Africa, Rome: FAO <ftp://ftp.fao.org/docrep/fao/009/a0782e/a0782e00.pdf>.

International Fund for Agricultural Development (IFAD) (2002) 'The rural poor', in *World Poverty Report 2001*, pp. 15–70, Rome: IFAD.

ICIPE (no date) 'Push–pull: A novel farming system for ending hunger and poverty in sub-Saharan Africa' [website] <www.push-pull.net/works.shtml> [accessed 15 November 2013].

IFAD (2009) 'Rural poverty in Kenya' [online] <www.ruralpovertyportal.org/web/guest/country/home/tags/kenya> [accessed 9 August 2013].

Kibue, M. (2007) 'Learning to set up a fair trade livestock marketing chain from Maasai pastoralists to consumers in Nairobi, Kenya' <www.future-agricultures.org/farmerfirst/files/T2c_Kibue.pdf> [accessed 1 August 2011].

Kinyanjui, M.N. (2010) 'Social relations and associations in the informal sector in Kenya', Social Policy and Development Programme – Paper No. 43, Geneva: United Nations Research Institute for Social Development <www.unrisd.org/80256B3C005BCCF9/(httpPublications)/E9CBDC63008BB214C12576DA00589211?OpenDocument> [accessed 15 November 2013].

Levidow, L. (2009) 'National policy context with potential relevance for AAFNs', FAAN Working Paper <www.faanweb.eu/sites/faanweb.eu/files/FAAN_D2_Policy_Context_AAFNs.pdf> [accessed 9 August 2013].

McIntyre, B.D., Herren, H.R., Wakhungu, J. and Watson, R.T. (eds) (2009) *Agriculture at a Crossroads: Global Report*, Washington, DC: International Assessment of Agricultural Knowledge, Science and Technology for Development, United Nations Environment Programme <www.unep.org/dewa/agassessment/reports/IAASTD/EN/Agriculture%20at%20a%20Crossroads_Global%20Report%20%28English%29.pdf> [accessed 9 August 2013].

Mehra, R. and Rojas, M.H. (2008) 'Women, food security and agriculture in a global marketplace', Washington, DC: International Centre for Research on Women <www.icrw.org/files/publications/A-Significant-Shift-Women-Food%20Security-and-Agriculture-in-a-Global-Marketplace.pdf> [accessed 9 August 2013].

Muchiri, S. and Kamau, M. (2011) 'Models of production', study paper for Eastern African Farmers Federation (EAFF), Nairobi.

Mulvany, P. and Ensor, J. (2011) 'Changing a dysfunctional food system: towards ecological food provision in the framework of food sovereignty', *Food Chain* 1 (1): 34–51 <http://dx.doi.org/10.3362/2046-1887.2011.004>.

Neondo, H. (2011) 'New approaches to an old technology prepare farmers in readiness to the impacts of climate change', *Africa Science News Service* <www.icipe.org/images/stories/pdf/news_and_events/2011/new_approaches_to_old_technology.pdf> [accessed 18 October 2013].

Nkendah, R. (2010) 'The informal cross-border trade of agricultural commodities between Cameroon and its CEMAC's neighbours', Paper for the NSF/AERC/IGC Conference, Mombasa, Kenya, 4 December.

Nyéléni (2007) Declaration and synthesis reports of 'Nyéléni 2007: Forum for Food Sovereignty' <www.nyeleni.org> [accessed 9 August 2013].

Nyéléni Europe (2012) 'Synthesis report and action plan', Forum for Food Sovereignty, 16–21 August 2011 in Krems/Austria <www.nyelenieurope.net/en/download> [accessed 9 August 2013].

Omiti, J., Otieno, D., McCullogh, E. and Nyanamba, T. (2008) 'Strategies to promote market-oriented smallholder agriculture in developing countries: a case of Kenya', in *AAAE Conference Proceedings* (2007), pp. 259–64 <http://purl.umn.edu/52105>.

Onduru, D. D, Gachimbi, L., De Jager, A., Gachini, G.N., Maina, F., and Muchena, F.N. (2002) 'Smallholder farming and rural livelihoods of central Kenya: a baseline survey of Kiambu District', INMASP Report No. 6.

ROPPA, EAFF and PROPAC (2011) 'Agricultural investment strengthening family farming and sustainable food systems in Africa,' Synthesis Report of the African farmer workshop, Yaoundé, Cameroon, 4–5 May <www.europafrica.info/en/publications/agricultural-investment-strengthening-family-farming-and-sustainable-food-systems-in-africa> [accessed 9 August 2013].

Stephens, E.C. and Barrett, C.B. (2006) 'Incomplete credit markets and commodity marketing behavior', Cornell University Working Paper, Ithaca, NY: Cornell University <http://dyson.cornell.edu/faculty_sites/cbb2/Papers/JAE%20resub%20Apr%202010%20with%20title%20page.pdf> [accessed 18 October 2013].

UK Food Group (UKFG) (2010) 'Securing future food: towards ecological food provision', UKFG <www.ukfg.org.uk/pdfs/Securing_future_food.pdf> [accessed 9 August 2013].

Watson D. J. and van Binsbergen J. (2008) 'Livestock market access and opportunities in Turkana, Kenya', ILRI Research Report 3, Nairobi, Kenya: International Livestock Research Institute.

World Health Organization (WHO) (2011) *Global Status Report on Noncommunicable Diseases*, Geneva: WHO <www.who.int/nmh/publications/ncd_report2010/en/> [accessed 11 October 2013].

Van Der Steen, D. (2010) 'The European CAP: history and evolution', in E. Calza Bini and S. Boccaleoni (eds), *Food Sovereignty: A Common Challenge in Africa and in Europe*, pp. 36–49, Rome: EuropAfrica Campaign.

europAfrica – Towards Food Sovereignty

europAfrica – Towards Food Sovereignty is a campaign that connects the African farmers' regional platforms and European civil society organisations to reflect and act together on major current issues concerning food and agricultural policies, trade and development cooperation. europAfrica aims to raise awareness and advocate on shared issues and to promote sustainable small-scale family farming and local agri-food systems that bring consumers and producers closer together. The campaign supports the realization of food sovereignty, i.e. the right for people and communities to define their own food and agricultural policies, both in Africa and in Europe, without impeding the food sovereignty of others.
More information: www.europafrica.info

The UK Food Group

The UK Food Group is the UK's principal civil society network on global food and farming issues. It brings together development, environment and farmers' groups in the UK working on global food, agriculture and hunger issues. The network's purpose is to strengthen advocacy in the UK for a global food system that can eradicate hunger, improve equity and restore the environment as part of achieving the Right to Food. It is the UK focal point for many European and International networks and represents BOND on these issues. The network also supports the emerging UK Food Sovereignty Movement.
More information: www.ukfg.org.uk